THE FREEWAY

The Freeway

A Play in Two Acts

by

PETER NICHOLS

FABER AND FABER
London · Boston

First published in 1975
by Faber and Faber Limited
3 Queen Square London WC1
Reprinted 1979
Printed in Great Britain by
Whitstable Litho Ltd Whitstable Kent
All rights reserved

ISBN 0 571 10744 3

All rights whatsoever in this play are strictly
reserved and applications for permission to perform
it, etc., must be made in advance, before
rehearsals begin, to Margaret Ramsay Ltd.,
14a Goodwin's Court, London WC2

Preface

The Great Traffic Jam is not a new theme. I first came across it in 1946 in James Hanley's strange novel, *What Farrar Saw*, which had been prompted by the thought of a return to pre-war motoring. J. G. Ballard has described the new landscape of motorways in a couple of recent novels. The cinema, which began by celebrating the car's infancy, has taken to abusing its old age in Fellini's *8½*, Godard's *Weekend* and Tati's *Traffic*. But *The Freeway* was, as far as I know, the first stage play to use the idea and, in view of its critical reception, may well be the last.

Most reviewers complained that the play wasn't horrible enough, but I don't think a jam would be all that nasty, even if it were allowed to happen. Far worse is our present reality—that almost every civilized requirement in town and country has been sacrificed to keep the traffic moving. "Now that we can travel easily," wrote Aldous Huxley, "we spend all our lives travelling." This urge for mobility has made the private car the most important single factor in advanced economies, East and West. The motor and haulage industries have pressed successive governments to adopt road-building programmes of such magnitude that nothing seems able to reverse the process. For a time, while I was writing this play, it appeared that the new petrol prices might do what no reasonable voice could and that *The Freeway* would be out of date before it was finished. But the North Sea oilfields mean that traffic levels will stay where they are till the local oil starts pouring through a few years from now. In other words, lorries built for continental autobahns will thunder through our narrow streets and rattle along the flyovers past curtained bedroom windows, commuters' cars will pour every morning into city centres the size of villages, and about 8,000 people will be killed each year on roads bearing one vehicle every twenty-four yards.

The more I thought and read about the traffic, the more it appeared that motors themselves aren't to blame, any more than aircraft could truly be said to have bombed Dresden. The real villain of this piece is the widely held conviction that the car is liberty incarnate, the great surviving champion of the free-for-all life-style. The motorist is persuaded to see the streets as something between the jungle and the Spanish Main, alive with Jaguars, Hunters, Thunderbirds, Corsairs, Mavericks and Rovers. Facing the usual barrage of red lights, crossings, lane markings and parking meters, is it any wonder that he can't see the connection? Or feels he's been robbed? There must be a better way. There is, but not many are prepared to consider it because it means co-operation. Allowing our towns and country to be wrecked is easier than voting for a rational transport system. The alternative to freedom is not necessarily a police state. The Nazis weren't the only people to get the trains running on time.

J. K. Galbraith has said that in cities Socialism is inevitable. In large towns, people aren't expected to dig their own drains, generate their own power or put out the fire when their houses burn. The solutions to these problems have been rational and co-operative. Why is the car such a diehard? I hope *The Freeway* suggests a few answers.

Anyone thinking of doing the play should be warned that, though set in the future, it is not an Orwellian nightmare. The world outside the jam seemed to me grisly enough without bringing tatty violence on to the stage. The mood is spring-like, a sunny weekend. There should be a colourful English landscape beyond the cars—pastiche-Constable—with a bright blue cyclorama which only darkens at the end. "A honeymoon bride", interviewed after an enormous traffic-jam in Florida, said: "It was like being stranded on a desert island with a lot of happy people."

Peter Nichols

"Paris" by François Nourissier
(from *Cartier-Bresson's France*, Thames & Hudson, London, 1971)

Parisians between them own a million cars. If to the city itself are added the three adjacent departments, which are in fact merely outer suburbs, the result is one car park of two million vehicles which has come into being in the twenty-five years since the Liberation. Every day 800,000 heedless suburban motorists come pouring into the city; whereas it is a proven fact that under normal conditions no more than 140,000 vehicles can circulate simultaneously in the central area. Stopping, parking in recognized parks or by the kerb is possible only for one car in two, not more. That is the equation. If some incident or circumstance, such as a storm, a public transport strike or the Friday-evening exodus, causes more than 140,000 out of the potential two million cars to take to the road at the same time, the city is blocked, jammed and brought to a standstill . . . !

. . . It is pointless to mince words: any talk about Paris in this moon-walking age is, first and foremost, talk about the motor car. Anything else is just literary froth, a privileged bird's-eye view. The piecemeal nature of authority, the absence of common sense and the passion for asserting individuality have all made their mark, so that life in Paris is now a real scourge.

One can disregard the more frivolous aspects of Paris, but this indigestible mass of sheet metal cannot be ignored. It sums up the situation. What is the point of writing about the pleasures of walking in the city when they are attended by nothing but risk and nasty smells? Or of waxing eloquent over the radiance of Paris, when the city's chief activity is reducing its unfortunate victims to nervous wrecks and exhausting its last gallant defenders?

Characters

LES LORIMER, 60
MAY, 60
WALLY, 60+
EVELYN, 60+
JAMES RHYNE, 55
NANCY, 75
GRANT SCALE, 25–30
TRACY, 25–30
COX, 40+
PAYNE, 20
NURSE, 18+
WATERMEN
BARRY POTTER, 50

A racing walker, stretcher-bearers, soldiers, security man, photographer, Scrubber, neighbours.

Radio voices.

The play was first presented by the National Theatre at the Old Vic in October 1974. The cast was as follows:

LES	Paul Rogers
MAY	Irene Handl
WALLY	Lionel Murton
EVELYN	Joan Hickson
JAMES	Graham Crowden
NANCY	Rachel Kempson
GRANT	Pip Miller
TRACY	Doran Godwin
COX	Antony Brown
PAYNE	Sara Van Beers
NURSE	Veronica Sowerby
BARRY	Mark Dignam

Directed by Jonathan Miller

Directions left and right read from actor's point of view.

A section of the approach-road to an inter-city freeway.

Downstage, between the audience and the main acting area, is a barbed-wire fence. Downstage of this a forestage.

The main area is a grass verge, sprinkled with paper and plastic containers. On either side are trees or shrubs for masking. On the right, also, a large road sign, facing the road at 45 degrees, so that we see only its plain back.

Some way upstage grass becomes road and on the road is a stationary queue of vehicles, facing right to left. Our view takes in the sides of three vehicles—or rather the whole of one in the middle and part of those on either side.

Left to right: an estate car, rear only; a Motor Home, the whole; a sports car, the front. The estate car is sober and British, the sports car foreign and fibreglass. The Motor Home is large, flashy and American-styled; has a window to the cab and a door with a window on its right. The rest of the side facing us is a plain panel, relieved by vents and Red Indian motifs. On the roof are sun panels and storage units. The single door facing us leads either to the driving cab or living quarters. Curtains can close off the windows.

Upstage of the road is more verge, another barbed-wire fence, then trees and sky, hillside and village, a traditional English landscape.

The vehicles, like the clothes, are imaginative developments of present styles.

The clothes of the Lorimer family are of synthetic fabrics in futuristic styles, contrasting both with their traditional interests and attitudes and with the Rhynes's clothes, which are arrogantly dowdy. The Scales are trendy but that, of course, may not mean modern.

ACT ONE

SCENE ONE

Morning.

House-lights dim and we hear the lowing of cows. This gives way soon to a chorus of motor-horns, beginning with one and rising to a climax.

At this, the curtain rises and for some moments the horns continue. LES LORIMER is standing or crouching beside his Motor Home polishing the bodywork. MAY, EVELYN and WALLY are sitting inside the driving cab, smoking and eating sweets, only partly seen.

If no curtain used, these four are in position while audience comes in; at first they sit waiting for traffic to move, then LES gets out to look, muttering with drivers from other cars, who come from upstage or off to look towards front of queue, left. There may be one or two horn-choruses during the half-hour before the house-lights go down. LES occupies the time more sensibly, polishing his vehicle.

LES is sixty or near it, once active, but growing fat through lack of exercise, speaks with London accent. He is always fiddling with some small manual job. He now looks up from his polishing towards the front of the queue, off left. Then he straightens up and looks again, as the chorus dies away. He turns and looks off, right. Then returns to the bodywork. MAY opens window.

MAY: Any sign of moving?

LES: Moving? The cars stretch out of sight both ways.

MAY: That many joined on behind?

LES: Coming all the time.

MAY: That case I think I'll stretch my legs.

> (*LES opens door and lets down the steps. She climbs down, speaking back into the bus.*)
> You two want a breath of air?

(WALLY *and* EVELYN *discuss it.* MAY *is a good-looking woman of fifty-five, but like her husband, putting on weight. She wears trousers and a tunic, has binoculars slung round her neck. Speaks with Welsh accent. She stands on grass, looks through glasses first left then right.*)

Seems to be solid right up to the Freeway. And look at them joining on the end every second. Blind as bats.

LES: *We* joined on the end. You don't know till it's too late. Then you can't back out. Ought to be a diversion.

MAY: *But those behind cried "Forward"*
And those before cried "Back!"

LES: Rest assured someone's trying to clear it. But blowing their horns like that is pointless. Childish. Making that row. Upset the animals.

MAY: Animals?
(*Searches with glasses.*)

LES: Somewhere beyond that fence.
(*She turns glasses towards audience and moves forward, peering at them.*)

MAY: Can't see any animals.

LES: You can hear them. Now and again. When the wind's in this direction.

MAY: Must be in those sheds.

LES: I told you we should have got away last night, avoid the Friday morning rush but no, you had to see the Pelota Championships . . .

MAY: I can see a farm-hand! I can see his white overall!
(WALLY *comes out, stretching, then gingerly climbs down steps. He's sixty, lean, wearing clothes in style of lumberjack or pioneer. Speaks with Canadian accent. He breathes deeply, filling his small chest and raising his arms. Pretends to cough.* MAY *laughs.*)

Every picture tells a story.
(WALLY *staggers and reels about, to show he is fainting from the fresh air.* LES *has finished cleaning the bus and looks at him without a smile.* EVELYN *laughs inside and* MAY *on the grass.* LES *shakes his head and goes into bus with dusters. They pause, then laugh again.*)

Laugh and the world laughs with you, cry and you cry
alone.

(WALLY *walks about and down to fence, looking around.*)

WALLY: This the Yorkshire National Park, Les? Don't see any
elephants.

MAY: Have to make do with cows.

WALLY: Don't see any cows either.

MAY: In those sheds down there.

(*She gives him glasses.*)

WALLY: Must be a dairy complex.

(*They look over audience for a moment.*)

British Columbia, they got this flock of chickens, they
bring them to all the country fairs, you know, the
neighbourhood fairs, for the kids to see. The old-fashioned
kind with the beaks left on.

MAY: That's nice, keeping up the old ways.

(LES *comes from bus with ciné-camera.*)

LES: Come on, Evelyn, don't you want to be in the film? Bring
a touch of glamour?

(*Winks at* MAY *and* WALLY. EVELYN *follows, sixty-two,
wearing elaborate blonde wig and safari suit. Moves sedately,
ladylike manner, smile fades at unpleasantness or nature.
Genteel London accent.*)

WALLY (*sings*): *Did you ever see a dream walking?*
               Well, I did . . .

EVELYN: Is there a breeze? D'you think my head needs a
dacron square?

MAY: Not a breath. It's a perfect day.

(EVELYN *at first holds her wig, then takes down hand and
moves gingerly across the verge.*)

EVELYN: Gracious, fancy being stranded here! The last place
God made.

LES: Don't come any further, Eve, by the bus is where I want
you.

(EVELYN *poses.* LES *lines up shot.*)

That's the style. Where the others? Come on, May, let's
be having you.

MAY: You didn't say you wanted me.

LES: Shouldn't have to say by now. Been taking you long enough.

MAY (*moving to join* EVELYN): Like a lamb to the slaughter.
(*The women link arms.*)

LES: Shouldn't have to tell you where to stand either. Not by this time. Where's Wally?
(WALLY *is at the fence, smoking a cigarette.*)

WALLY: Me too?

LES: It's your holiday! Blimey O'Riley! You want a cinématic record! Think I'm doing this for my own amusement?

WALLY: How about me walking over and you kinda following with the camera?

LES: What for?

WALLY: That's a movie-camera you got there!

LES: Leave the photography to me, all right? The last shot I had on here was—what? D'you remember?

WALLY: I guess not.

LES: Anyone?
(*The women can't either.*)
No. Well, it's all in here!
(*Taps his head.*)
That's the difference, see? It was a slow pan across the pedestrian precinct at Green Park. Finishing with you lot feeding the ducks.

MAY: Oh, yes—

LES: And now you're saying another follow-shot the opposite way? You want to make your Canadian friends all giddy? Show them a film with nothing but shots of you on the move, they'll be getting a false impression!
(*Laughs. So do women.*)
They'll say "Gee, Wally, didn't they give you no rest over in l'il old England?"
(WALLY *joins the women.* LES *lines up again.*)
Closer to Eve, you're off frame. Not too close, don't stand behind her. I've lost you altogether now.

MAY (*sings*): *Stand up, stand up for Jesus,*
The beggars at the back can't see!

LES: That's better. Give us a smile then. This is only a camera,

14

not a missile-launcher. Look as though you're enjoying
  yourselves.

EVELYN: Chance to do some acting.

LES: Here we go!

WALLY: Roll 'em!

  (*They smile and stand motionless while* LES *runs the camera.*)

MAY: A picture no artist could paint.

LES: It's not a talkie, thank you.

  (*After some time,* TRACY SCALE *comes on from sports car,
  right. She is in late twenties, her real prettiness almost hidden
  by a trendy outfit—perhaps a Mao tunic and black cap with
  huge dark glasses. Something of that sort anyway. We can see
  that she has a good figure too.*)

MAY: Look out!

TRACY: Sorry.

LES (*taking down camera*): That's ruined that shot.

TRACY: Very sorry, I didn't see.

LES: Can't be helped.

TRACY: Only going to meet my husband.

EVELYN: He been up to have a look?

TRACY: That's right.

LES: To the Freeway?

TRACY: Well, I mean, how long are we expected to wait here?
  I've got two young children in that Kamikaze.

LES: They'll get us through as soon as possible.

MAY: Can we break away now, Les?

LES: I should, if I were you.

MAY: Stuck here like cheese at fourpence.

  (MAY, WALLY *and* EVELYN *move away and* LES *stows camera
  as* GRANT *comes on from left, wearing expensive jungle-green
  or camouflage suit, boots, dark glasses. Like* TRACY, *has slight
  London suburban accent.*)

TRACY: Well, did you get there?

GRANT: Yes.

TRACY: Do we look like moving?

GRANT: No way.

LES: What seems to be the trouble?

GRANT: Everyone tells a different story.

LES: Then it's not just an everyday super pile-up?

GRANT: They'd have cleared that by now.

LES: What I thought.

GRANT: Every lane's solid, far as you can see, both ways.

TRACY: Both ways?

GRANT: The kids all right?

TRACY: All right so far. Sholto's gone to sleep and Stephanie's modelling a rabbit.

GRANT: Might as well picnic now, save time later.

TRACY: Right. Hope we're not too late at Mother's, she gets jittery.

GRANT: Give her an interbuzz if we're held up long.

TRACY: Right!

(She goes off to their car. He opens boot, which is bonnet, takes out picnic and goes after her.)

WALLY *(watching them)*: They're going to have themselves a spot of chow.

(MAY has gone left and is looking off through glasses. EVELYN sits on step of bus. WALLY turns back to LES.)

What d'you say, Les? Spot of chow? Good idea—

LES: If they threw themselves under a bus, would you follow suit?

MAY: Difference between scratching your head and pulling all the hair out.

LES: Mind out, Evelyn.

EVELYN *(on step, in his way)*: Consider yourself squashed.

LES: How's that?

EVELYN: Wally was only making a suggestion. There's no call to bite his head off.

LES: Fair enough, get out the chairs and tables, cook the dinner. What if this lot suddenly clears, d'you expect me to hold up all those cars while you lot get the equipment back in the Cherokee?

(EVELYN stands and moves away to WALLY, who is now at fence.)

EVELYN: Let's you and I console ourselves with a menthol.

(They light up cigarettes.)

May! D'you care for a menthol?

16

MAY: If we can't eat, we may as well smoke ourselves to death.
  (*Joins them as* WALLY *coughs.*)
LES: We could have some *elevenses*.
EVELYN: We had some elevenses at half-past nine.
WALLY: That was half-past nineses.
LES: That was coffee. We could have some tea.
EVELYN: We *could*. We haven't had tea since breakfast.
LES: Wally, come on, stir your stumps.
  (*Goes back into bus.* WALLY *moves to bus.*)
WALLY: No rest for the wicked.
MAY (*sings*): *I like a nice cup of tea in the morning* . . .
  (*She follows* LES *into bus.*

  JAMES RHYNE *comes from upstage of the estate car, left. He
  opens the boot with a key and rummages inside, producing a
  plaid blanket. He comes down to the grass verge and clears a
  few square feet of litter. He is fifty-five, attentive, extremely
  courteous. Bewildered by techniques of all kinds, he is at home
  with words and ideas, immensely appreciative of others'
  qualities. Speech, often hurried, indistinct; the diction of a
  gent. He is wearing dinner-jacket, black tie, etc. Having
  cleared a space, he spreads the blanket on the ground.
  He is followed by* NANCY, *seventy-five, a dowager with a
  grand manner but a bark worse than her bite. She can be put
  down by her son's quiet insistence on the true state of affairs.
  She carries an elegant container. Kicks aside more rubbish.
  She is wearing a rather dowdy evening dress and an unbecoming
  perm.*)
NANCY: Were I ever asked for the most emblematic feature of
  modern Britain, I should point to her ill-kept verges.
JAMES: Executed by you, Mother, that could hardly fail to be an
  impressive gesture. However, I'm sure you're aware that the
  likelihood of your being asked is extremely remote. You're
  not exactly *vox pop*.
  (*They sit on the blanket and during this* NANCY *opens the
  container and takes out a thermos flask and two mugs. She
  pours coffee and offers a biscuit.*)
NANCY: You persist in that opinion against all evidence to the
  contrary.

JAMES: What evidence, Mother?

(LES *has come from bus, with a cylindrical device like a kettle and some newspapers.* MAY, EVELYN *and* WALLY *are watching the* RHYNES.)

LES: Get weaving, Wally.

WALLY: That the paper?

LES: Yeah. You got to tear it up.

(LES *returns to bus while* WALLY *sets the kettle on the verge and tears the newspaper into shreds, stuffing the pieces into the open top.* EVELYN *helps him, tearing the paper while he lights the shreds in the kettle.*)

NANCY: I'm often stopped in the street, for my views on this and that. The state of the nation. The place of drugs in the modern Church. Do I think Nagasaki Knickers are too revealing? Not revealing enough?

JAMES: I'm sure they *ask* you, Mother. That's not in dispute. In a count of heads, yours would serve as well as another. I'm only making the point that you are not exactly An Average Housewife.

NANCY: I hope I'll never be seen as an average anything.

WALLY: Is the water in?

LES: Yes. You only got to boil it.

JAMES: When someone says Old Age Pensioner, your image is not the first that springs to mind.

NANCY: You, on the other hand, rather fancy yourself as The Man in the Street. A freeman of the caste system moving freely acrawse the divisive boundaries or whatever they are.

(LES *brings folding table and chairs from bus and begins to erect them on the verge.*

JAMES *offers* NANCY *the biscuits and she chooses.*)

JAMES: I'm not sure what you mean by a freeman of the caste system. And I'm not sure you're sure either. As long as——

NANCY: I'm very clear what I mean——

JAMES: Mother, please, will you allow me to finish? As long as you don't mean I'm a sycophantic creep of some kind, then I accept the definition, with some reservations.

(MAY *comes from bus with tray, on which are set melamine cups, saucers, a teapot, biscuits, sugar, milk, etc., puts tray on table and lays them out.*)

MAY (*to the world in general*): They also serve who only stand and wait.

(EVELYN *helps while* WALLY *struggles with kettle and* LES *opens chairs.* NANCY *glances at them.*)

NANCY: Everything but the kitchen sink. And I suppose *that's* in the bus. Or whatever they call it.

JAMES: The Motor Home.

NANCY: I thought you'd know.

(WALLY *is creating clouds of black smoke with his burning newspaper.* MAY *waves it away.*)

MAY (*sings*): There's a silver lining
     Through the dark clouds shining—

LES: What's up, Wally? Spot of bother with the Vesuvius?

(*He goes to help.* NANCY *coughs pointedly and* MAY *looks at them nervously.*)

MAY: Sorry about the smoke.

JAMES (*half-rising*): I absolutely hadn't noticed.

(*He sits again.* EVELYN *takes teapot to kettle and* WALLY *pours in the water, now hot.* LES *moves to* JAMES *and* NANCY, *smiling and making faces towards his family.*)

LES: Talk about Fred Karno's Army.

JAMES (*rising again*): I beg your pardon?

LES: I say, talk about an awkward squad.

JAMES: I was about to praise your impressive *esprit de corps*. (*And quickly enlarging, explaining:*) Everyone with a job to do.

LES: I try to keep them up to scratch. No margin for error when you're halfway across Bulgaria.

JAMES: No indeed.

LES: Or up the Pyrenees.

MAY: When you see a vacant place at a lay-by, you've got to grab it.

(*She pours milk into each cup.*)

LES: But our drill's bound to be a bit rough today. We got a raw recruit. My wife's brother over from Canada. We're showing him the sights. And teaching him to boil the Vesuvius.

(EVELYN *comes to table with teapot and stirs.* WALLY *stands and puts cork into kettle.*)

You finished with the bonfire, Wally?

(*Laughs and winks at* JAMES.)

JAMES: Are you Northward bound?

LES: Only as far as Yorkshire National Park. See the dolphins at Fountains Abbey. We thought of nipping up to the Braemar Games after but this means our schedule's gone for a burton. And we only got food and water for a day, so I reckon we'll have to make do with Hadrian's Wall, stay overnight, then off back home tomorrow afternoon.

MAY: Oh yes, let's see the Wall. (*To* JAMES.) I've been taking Roman Britain in evening class.

LES: Always got her nose in some historical novel.

MAY: I like anything hysterical.

(*She laughs and goes to help* EVELYN *pour tea.* WALLY *comes, wiping hands.*)

JAMES: As an experienced traveller, what's your view of the situation? Would you hazard an informed guess at the outcome?

LES: What, the jam? Couldn't say. Got to sit tight. Grin and bear it.

JAMES: That would be your general approach? Remain calm?

LES: Definitely. No use blowing horns, for instance. Childish. Making a row won't help.

JAMES: I can't tell you how heartily I agree. However, the futility of such gestures should not be advanced as a reason for preventing them. The right to make futile gestures is an inalienable part of our way of life. A thread in the intricate pattern of freedom. We must trust that wiser counsels will prevail.

MAY: Tea up! Them as wants it come and get it.

(*The two men have been standing centre, the others sitting and pouring, eating, etc.*)

LES: Lorimer's the name. Les Lorimer.

(JAMES *had thought the conversation over and was returning to sit by his mother. He stands again and comes to shake hands.)*

JAMES: How d'you do? James Rhyne. (*Pronounced "Reen".*)

LES: My wife May.

MAY (*stretching across* LES *to shake hands with* JAMES): Excuse me retching, I've just come off the boat.

JAMES: My mother.

LES (*crossing to her*): You all right on the ground, Mrs. Rhyne?

NANCY: Perfectly, thank you.

LES: Only if you'd like to share our furniture, Wally can easy sit on the verge.

NANCY: Most kind of you but this is what I'm used to.

LES: Hoping to go far?

NANCY: Ross eventually. Ross and Cromarty.

JAMES: Scotland.

LES: For the skiing or what?

NANCY: The stalking.

LES (*not understanding*): Oh, yes.

NANCY: Lest you should think us unsuitably clad, I ought to explain that our first call will be at the Tithe Barn Festival. *Mary Stuart.* Donizetti. Though it seems unlikely now, that this will clear in time for the overture. If I tell the truth, the picnic's the part I most enjoy.
(LES *knows no more than before she started.* MAY *draws* JAMES *towards the table where* EVELYN *and* WALLY *are sitting.*)

MAY: My colleague, Evelyn.

JAMES: How d'you do? You did say "colleague"?

EVELYN: We're in the same dragshop. I'm on the wig counter, May's in the knitwear.

MAY: And my kid brother, Wally.

WALLY: Hi!

JAMES: Seeing plenty of changes?

WALLY: Thirty years since I was here, it's changed all right.

JAMES: And getting wonderful weather.

MAY: I told him, he must have brought the sunshine in his suitcase.

JAMES: Yes indeed! Well, if you'll excuse me—

LES (*returning to meet him*): This pantomime with the Vesuvius,

that's not usual. Primitive. Wasteful. Pollutes the environment. No, we normally have hot water on tap in the
Cherokee. You seen one of these jobs, have you?

JAMES: Your Motor Home? Most impressive!

LES: If we're stuck here long, I'll give you the guided tour.

JAMES: Would it be any trouble?

LES: Say the word.

JAMES: Most grateful.

(MAY, EVELYN *and* WALLY *are at table drinking tea.*)

LES: Got a hundred-litre storage tank with twenty thousand
B.T.U. heating and air conditioning throughout. Just at
the moment, though, she's having one or two teething
troubles. The recirculating toilet's leaking into the water
system and the refrigerator thermostat's on the blink.

MAY: You can cut the milk with a saw.

LES: So we've had to bring water in a jerrican. Only natural the
first year.

JAMES: Really?

LES: Since they rationalised inspection.

JAMES: You seem extremely well-informed.

LES: Spent most of my life in a motor works. Started on the
shop-floor and finished on the staff. *Works* staff, mind you.
Still a working man.

NANCY: James! Your coffee will be cold.

MAY: And your tea.

LES (*winking at* JAMES): In the dog-house.

JAMES: Absolutely.

(*Smiles and they return to their drinks. On the road upstage
people pass back and forth, looking at their vehicles, etc.,
occasionally travellers go by on the grass, downstage, by the
fence.*

Two Autoguards enter. COX, *the man, is a middle-aged
servant, reassuring, avuncular. He has the slow and deliberate
demeanour of a gardening expert or cricket commentator.
His uniform has many features taken from the old motoring
clubs: boots, breeches, Sam Browne belts, peaked caps.* PAYNE,
*the woman, is young, scrubbed, fresh, everyone's ideal nurse.
She has an outfit which uses same colour scheme as* COX's *but*

22

has features taken from those of air hostesses, meter maids, police-women. They enter up right.)

COX (*saluting casually*): Morning, all.

(At first they treat only with the LORIMERS, *not seeing the* RHYNES.)*

LES: Good morning, officer.

COX: Lovely morning.

LES: Not too bad.

COX: Sort of weather makes you thankful to be in good old England. Not rotting away in some prison camp.

LES: Any news from the front?

PAYNE: Only just arrived on duty, haven't we, Sarge? They've told us nothing.

COX: We're as much in the dark as you are, friend.

PAYNE: Nobody ever tells you anything, do they, Sarge?

COX: That's enough cheek from you, young Payne. Some of these young Guardettes, they get above themselves. (*Winks at* LORIMERS.) Any more and I shall take you across my knee. I'm still big enough.

PAYNE: I'd like to see you try.

COX: Watch your step, young lass, or you'll find out.

(LORIMERS laugh at all this, as at a much-loved television series.)

PAYNE: All right, Sergeant, I'll come quietly.

COX: Cheeky young article. (*Laughs warmly.*)

PAYNE: Well this won't get the membercards checked. Can we see your card, sir?

WALLY: Oh, I don't have one. I'm Canadian.

PAYNE: Haven't you got a Canadian membercard?

WALLY: I'm not a motorist.

LES: He's my passenger.

(Offers membercard, which COX scrutinises.)

PAYNE: You ladies associate members?

MAY: I am.

EVELYN: I only go on the Freeway in their car. It's hardly worth me joining.

PAYNE (*offering brochures*): You can't have read our literature.

COX: All right, Mr. Lorimer. (*Punches card with register which*

23

bleeps.)

EVELYN: I can't really afford it, dear, since my hubby passed away.

PAYNE: But don't you think you *should* afford it? After all, you use the Freeway——

EVELYN: Only when they take me out——

PAYNE: —you're happy to take advantage of all that's been achieved so far in the motorist's struggle against victimisation——

EVELYN (*cornered*): It's a free country!

COX: Steady on there. Take it easy, young Payne, you get a bit hot under the collar. What I think my young friend's trying to say is that this is only a free country because we make it so.

PAYNE: Those who are not for us are against us.

COX: Your name will be turning up on one of those pedestrian petitions. You mark my words.

EVELYN: I've never joined anything. I never have. I've never voted. I never would.

COX: You can't be sure. *Some*body signs them. Somebody wants to clear city centres of private cars. It's not me. It's not Mr. Lorimer here.

LES: I've talked till I'm blue in the face. Women can't grasp politics.

(COX *moves to* RHYNES *and takes* JAMES's *card.*)

PAYNE: You have a think. Consider the benefits. For only half the annual subscription you receive a free badge which makes you an Associate Freewoman and once a month a free copy of our magazine, *Free-for-all*, which includes features on fashion, showbiz and ecology, with many free offers and exciting new competitions.

COX (*handing back* JAMES's *card*): Thank you, my lord.

(*Everyone looks at* JAMES.)

JAMES: Sarnt. What information can you give us?

COX: Precious little, my lord.

JAMES: But surely something must be known about this delay.

COX: It seems to have begun with a routine pile-up but now, with more cars joining on the end all the time——

JAMES: But there appears to be no movement at all. Can't the obstruction be cleared? Correct me if I'm wrong—I understood that mobile casualty stations could be on the spot within ten minutes.

COX: That's true, my lord, up to a point.

NANCY: Up to a point, Sergeant? Sergeant—?

COX (*saluting*): Cox, my lady.

(PAYNE *has crossed to join the* RHYNES. MAY *and* EVELYN *clear tea-things into bus.*)

NANCY: Up to what point?

COX: Well, the truth of the matter is we're a bit understaffed at the moment and the patrols already had one incident to cope with on the same stretch of Freeway. A lot of metal-cutting and some tricky amputations.

PAYNE: Can be difficult. The welders jostling the anaesthetists. TV cameras nudging the surgeon's arm.

NANCY: D'you think we can be in Yorkshire by half past four?

PAYNE: I wouldn't bank on it, madam.

NANCY: We'd better skip the Donizetti and get straight up to Edinburgh.

JAMES: Forgive me, Sarnt, if I appear to be teaching my grandmother to suck eggs, but shouldn't you and your fellow guards be preventing more cars joining on the end of the line?

LES: They ought to be diverted on to the old motorways and A-roads—

(EVELYN *and* MAY *have been clearing away the tea-things during the last dialogue.* WALLY *has fallen asleep in his seat.* COX *ignores* LES.)

COX: Now, now, now, my lord, keep your shirt on. Over the past few years the British motorist has weathered a good few crises, what with our Arab friends; and the unions . . . but one way or another he's kept on the move. Oh, there may be some rotten apples amongst them but your average Autoclubman is steady, independent, not easily roused but when he is, watch out, you'll find he won't let go in a hurry –

25

(*Breaks off, takes out handkerchief and blows nose.*)

PAYNE (*putting her hand on his arm*): Sarge—

COX: All right, young Payne, I know. (*Then gruffly.*) We'd best be cutting along.

PAYNE (*to* EVELYN): I'll leave you this free copy of *Free-for-all*. See if it changes your mind about joining. And if you decide to, that's my number on the cover. Quote that and your application will be dealt with personally by my own computer.

EVELYN: Thanks very much.

COX: Anything you want, my lord, give us a shout . . . my lady.

(*They both salute.*)

NANCY: Good-day, Sergeant. Keep us informed.

(*Guards make towards right.* PAYNE *goes but* COX *turns.*)

COX: Morning, all. Mind how you go.

(*Suddenly the loud battering sound of an approaching helicopter. Everyone looks up, following its course from left to right. Other travellers, passing along the road between vehicles, pause to watch it pass.* COX *goes off. The wind of the propellers blows the grass as the helicopter goes over.* WALLY *wakes suddenly, stands, realises what it is. The noise and wind die away.*)

NANCY: Military, Autoclub or what?

LES: Media, TV.

NANCY: Theirs would be first.

JAMES: Therein lies our safety, Mother. The broadcasting of uncensored views and information.

LES: Looks as though we'll be here for a good while yet.

NANCY: We may as well eat.

LES: Have to scrub round Fountains Abbey. That all right, Wally?

WALLY: How's that, Les?

LES: I say: scrub round the dolphinarium.

WALLY: Sure. They got dolphins over there. When you seen one dolphin you seen 'em all.

JAMES: Will you bring the basket, Mother? I'll see to the wine.

(*They make towards their estate car, taking their coffee-*

cups, etc. MAY *has come from bus, with a dinky apron like* EVELYN'*s.*

LES *signals to them to follow downstage. He glances at the* RHYNES.)

LES: D'you hear what the Sergeant called them?

MAY (*to* WALLY): You never expected to meet the gentry.

LES: That's not much of a car for a lord and lady. Flat tyre, too, by the look of it.

EVELYN: You'd think they hadn't got two pee to rub together.

WALLY: Maybe they've happened on hard times?

MAY: They dress the part anyway.

EVELYN: But if that dress was the best I could afford, I should die of shame! It might be made of furnishing fabric!
(*From offstage right, hear* GRANT, TRACY *and their two children singing 'I'm a Suitcase'.*)

MAY: Oh look, that couple in the next car, they're having a sing-song with their kiddies. We used to have to do that with ours on long journeys, d'you remember, Les?
(RHYNES *begin to return and* LORIMERS *break up.*)

EVELYN: Dinner's nearly ready. May put it on when she heard that Autoguard—

LES: Might as well have lunch, yes, why not?

MAY: That's a relief: my stomach thinks my throat's cut.

LES: All right. The more practice Wally gets, the easier it'll be on the Continent.
(NANCY *brings modest picnic basket and sits on rug, taking out a good deal of traditional cold fare: meats, salad, Stilton, fruit and bread, all of which they eat with their hands.*

LES *fetches clip-board and whistle from bus. He checks stopwatch, gives starting whistle. Women go into bus and* LES *hangs clip-board on bus.*

LES *and* WALLY *unscrew fittings on lower part of bodywork, unfolding hinged section, perhaps half of wall facing us. They lift this until it becomes an awning. They detach two poles clamped inside and plant them in ground.*

Revealed are MAY *and* EVELYN *at the vinyl fittings of their ideal kitchen: in upstage wall are a sink, eye-level grill and two burners with pans simmering; fridge; etc.* MAY *attends to*

27

steaks, hammering and trimming.

EVELYN *switches on her radio, which plays a jaunty number from the Tijuana Brass, which continues as music for the sequence.*

WALLY *brings a rush mat from bus and* LES *kicks aside paper rubbish and directs* WALLY *to unroll mat where he's cleared, a position right of centre.* MAY *comes from bus with a battery-operated dustette and vacuums the mat.* LES *and* WALLY *then move table on to mat and place chairs round it.*

Now the central area is clear, RHYNES *picnicking one side,* LORIMERS *the other.*

JAMES *has returned, brings bottle of claret, which he stands opening.* NANCY *takes glasses from basket and in due course they pour and drink.*

EVELYN *comes from bus with laden tray.* MAY *takes a plastic cloth from it, with a hole in the centre. She lays this on the table, then* EVELYN *puts tray on it. They lay four settings with glasses, paper napkins, pepper and salt, table mats.*

LES *has gone round the bus to the upstage side, right.* WALLY *goes to consult the clip-board, putting on glasses to read it, taking them off afterwards. He follows* LES *as* LES *emerges on top, opens storage unit and passes things down to* WALLY, *who returns downstage with a bright canvas sunshade.* EVELYN *to bus with tray.* MAY *goes back to bus with dustette.* WALLY *opens umbrella and shows a large shade with a short pole. He holds it above him, then puts pole through central hole of table. Umbrella rests on table, covering the surface. He puts hands on hips and looks at it, on top and underneath.* EVELYN *comes from bus with plastic pedal-bin, puts it near bus.* LES *comes from upstage with a canvas bag. Passing* WALLY, *he sees umbrella, pauses, throws an extension pole on to ground, passes on.* EVELYN *helps* WALLY *take out umbrella and fix extension pole, put it back through hole in table.*

LES *throws contents of bag on to ground, down right: canvas, metal poles, pegs. He begins to sort them.* MAY *from bus with tray of bowls, tin, tin-opener, bread in packet and bread-basket,* EVELYN *goes to bus.* MAY *takes sliced bread from packet and arranges it in basket, then pours fruit salad from tin into*

28

bowls, four portions. Perhaps cream too? WALLY *goes to look at rota and enters bus, as* EVELYN *comes out with plastic vase and polythene bag, goes to table.*

LES *is erecting a toilet-tent downstage, first piecing frame together, then sorting canvas.*

RHYNES *eat, drink, and watch with interest.* EVELYN *takes from bag plastic flowers and puts them in vase, puts bag on tray, which* MAY *now returns to bus, as* WALLY *comes out with a spiked stick.* MAY *drops empty fruit tin into pedal-bin, then goes into bus.* WALLY *begins picking up plastic and paper debris from whole area, putting it into plastic bin at intervals.* EVELYN *goes into bus and* MAY *comes out with wine bottle, corkscrew and cheeseboard. Puts all on table.* EVELYN *reappears with folding washstand and plastic bowl to fit; erects this near door of bus.*

WALLY *leaves spike near bus and reads rota again. Bell rings once offstage and* MAY *reacts, hurrying off to bus.* WALLY *goes round it upstage and off. The whistle of a boiling kettle sounds and* EVELYN *hurries into bus.* MAY *comes from bus with hot vegetable dish, which she puts on table.* EVELYN *then comes with kettle of hot water, which she pours into the washbowl.* WALLY *comes from upstage, rear, with a chemical lavatory seat and bucket. Takes it down to tent and looks for* LES, *who indicates that he put bucket down and help* LES *finish tent. This they do.*

Bell offstage rings twice and MAY *runs back to bus.* WALLY, *hammering in a tent peg with a mallet, hurts his finger and backs away, sucking it, shaking it, etc.*

EVELYN *comes down to him, but* LES *goes on working, ignoring him. Bell offstage rings three times and* EVELYN *has to run, meeting* MAY *coming out with second vegetable dish.* WALLY *makes to go on helping* LES, *but* LES *points upstage and* WALLY *goes.* LES *gets tent finished and goes inside with the lavatory.* MAY *finds room on table for dish and* WALLY *goes upstage of bus.*

EVELYN *reappears with a box with a red cross on it but seeing no* WALLY *returns to bus with it.*

WALLY *comes from upstage of bus with chemicals in plastic*

jars, goes into tent with them.

    EVELYN *comes from bus with two plates and two steaks.* LES *goes up to washbowl and washes hands.* MAY, *seeing this, runs into bus, as* EVELYN *puts out steaks on two plates and sets them on table.* MAY *comes out with handful of paper towels just in time for* LES *to wipe his hands, afterwards disposing of towel in pedal-bin.*

    Bell offstage rings four times and MAY *goes to answer.*

    WALLY *backs out of tent, goes to rota, checks it.* LES *takes position at table, removes cork from bottle.* EVELYN *takes off apron, goes into bus as* MAY *reappears with two more plates and steaks, which she sets on table.*

    LES *pours wine in each glass.* EVELYN *comes with radio and takes seat.* MAY *removes her apron and takes it into bus,* WALLY *washes his hands and looks for towels as* MAY *comes again, showing them. He wipes his hands.* MAY *sits at table.* LES *looks at his watch, then at* WALLY, *who hurries to take his place.*

    EVELYN *stops radio music.* LES *looks at watch, blows whistle. Silence.*)

LES: Not too bad. I suppose we can't expect miracles. Everyone got their Liebfraumilch?
    (*They raise their glasses.*)
    Buon appetito!

OTHERS: Skol, cheers, bottoms up, etc. . . .
    (JAMES *is watching and* LES *sees him.* LES *raises his glass.* JAMES *half-rises from the ground.*)

JAMES: Your very good health.
    (EVELYN'*s radio is on the ground beside her. She switches it on at once, and to the music of the Tijuana Brass, the* LORIMER *family help themselves to vegetables.*

    Lights plunge to black. Music continues as both sets of picnics are cleared.)

During change, hear media voice on speakers.

NEWSMAN: The Autoclubs report that travellers on the Royal
   Freeway may experience some delay. The cause is
   apparently another demonstration by the Scrubbers, the
   anti-motor group whose avowed aim is to paralyse the
   Freeway. The incident began with two ordinary collisions,
   each involving less than thirty vehicles, but rescuers
   arrived to find the terrorists already occupying the wreckage.
   Mobile mercy teams were given access to clear the dead
   and wounded although the Scrubbers have remained in
   position, blocking the Northbound Freeway, chanting
   slogans and, as these pictures show, exposing their private
   parts to the watching newsmen.
   (*Light gradually shows the same scene, now lit by the moon.
   Several other sources of light. The kitchen panel of the bus
   is now closed.* JAMES *is rummaging in the boot of his car with
   a gazlamp;* LES *is lying on the ground by the* RHYNES' *car,
   looking at the tyre by torchlight.*
   The furniture is as it was.
   JAMES *emerges with a bottle and a cigar box, crosses to
   table and puts them there, leaving the gazlamp there too.
   He is still wearing dinner jacket. Now the announcement comes
   from the bus.*)
   A spokesman says the situation is not so far regarded as
   serious, though travellers are advised to avoid the Freeway
   and its linkroads. Those with unavoidable journeys might,
   at their own risk, try exploring the old A-roads and
   motorways. In this case, drivers should be armed and are
   advised to keep their windows firmly closed against
   marauding bands of lorry-drivers.
   (JAMES *returns to his car and takes out some glasses.*)
JAMES: You will, of course, let me know if there's anything at
   all I can do to help?
LES: Not at the moment.

NEWSMAN: At Royal Albert Hall, the gold medal in the
International Pelota Championship went to Duk Soo
Chung of Korea for the third year running . . .
(*Hear the viewers groaning.*)

JAMES (*bending slightly to show concern*): Is it serious? Will it be
a tremendous job?

LES: Only a matter of changing a wheel. Still you don't want to
waste time stopping at the next oasis. I'll change it for you
in the morning. Easier in daylight.

JAMES: I'm extremely obliged to you.

LES (*standing and showing him*): The bodywork's had a bash
here, see, your wing's been rubbing against the wheel.
We shall have to pull that out a bit. D'you remember it
happening?

JAMES: Yes, indeed. A container-truck went into the back as
my wife was waiting at the lights. Yes, that's right, the
driver jumped out at once and started hammering on her
roof with his fist and kicking the door and shouting at her
in Italian.

LES: Going through his accident drill.

JAMES: Precisely.

LES: As laid down by the Intercontinental Haulage Combines.

JAMES: Quite so.
(*Together they walk towards the table.*)
Les, this hardly seems a recompense for the sweat of your
brow, but I hope you'll give me the pleasure of accepting
a cigar?

LES: I won't say no, thanks very much.

JAMES: And some Armagnac?
(LES *stares until* JAMES *shows the flask.*)
I fear by your expression that Cognac is your drink.
Foolishly I have none with me, though you may enjoy
Armagnac almost as much.

LES: Kind of brandy, is it? Fair enough.
(*As they talk,* JAMES *lights his cigar and pours them each a
drink.* LES *sips.*)

JAMES: Is it in any way comparable to what you're used to?

LES: Japanese, is it?

JAMES: Only French, I fear.

LES: Not bad. Not bad at all. Very nice. No, as I say, these kind of teething troubles, only natural the first year, now they've handed inspection over to the customer.

JAMES: How fascinating! Do enlarge on that point.

LES: Well, inspection used to be a time-wasting process. Then somebody with brains invented the warranty. See, what they call a warranty is only saying: you find the faults and we'll repair them free.

JAMES: The advantage to the customer being—?

LES: To keep down costs.

JAMES: Of course.

LES: After a year the vehicle's usually over the worst. From then on it's trouble-free motoring all the way. Only snag is changing ours every year we tend to lose the benefit. Still, common sense to change every twelve month, good part-exchange, up-to-date refinements.

JAMES: I must say it's extremely reassuring to hear this policy of rapid obsolescence upheld by a man with such vast experience. I'm afraid it's had the usual mud slung at it by the lefties.

LES: I wouldn't say 'vast'.

JAMES: All your working life? One man can't do more.

LES: I'd like to show you something, James.
(*Goes to bus as* WALLY *comes out*.)
Anything on the news?
(*Goes in without waiting for reply*.)

WALLY: They reckon it's some fellows called the Scrubbers are at the back of it.
(*Sits at table*.)

JAMES: I might have known.

WALLY: Who are they?

JAMES: A group of simple-minded extremists. They have youth on their side and the sentimental appeal of push-bicycles and canal barges but so far they enjoy no broad popular support.

WALLY: They got them over in B.C. Same shaven heads but a different name. They call them Greenhorns.

33

JAMES: Scrubber was originally a pejorative term which they— and their P.R. people—have shrewdly embraced. Rather as the Methodists and Quakers did,—

WALLY: And the Tories.

JAMES (*laughing*): Precisely! Now, Wally, will you give me the pleasure of accepting a brandy?

WALLY: Fine, thank you.

JAMES: And a cigar?

WALLY: Why not?

JAMES: Marvellous.

(LES *comes from bus to find* WALLY *being waited on*.)

LES (*puts on table a photograph album and himself sits*): There you are, James! A photographic record of my working life presented to me free, gratis and for nothing by the Ford company to mark the completion of my fortieth year.

WALLY: D'you really think he should see it, Les? That's pretty hot stuff.

LES: You'll have to pardon the smell of sour grapes coming off my brother-in-law. He was on the shop-floor too—

WALLY: Over there—

LES: Even a steward. But he couldn't stay the course. So now he's struggling along in retirement with only the old-age pension. Not even got a car.

WALLY: I *never* had a car——

LES (*over this*): As you see, James, we start with group pictures of the lads on the floor. Before the war these. Tell by the haircuts.

JAMES: You in the back row there?

LES: Just got my face in, see? Metal Stamping and Body Division, that is. And there's the lads from Enamel Booths. Wet deck there. Engine Dress. And that's outside the welding shop, on the forecourt, where we used to play soccer before they made it into a car-park. Well, nobody *had* a car in those days. What we call the dark ages.

JAMES: Ah, now you're in the front row, with a white coat.

WALLY (*sings*): *The working class*
      Can kiss my arse
      I've got the foreman's job at last.

LES (*to him*): That may be some supervisors' attitude but not mine.

WALLY: They bought you off with a white coat.

LES: I never lost my sympathy with the lads. I knew life on the line. I'd seen the struggles we had just to get control of the key.

JAMES: The key? To what?

LES: To control the speed of the line. There's a rate for the job laid down by management. So many cars an hour.

WALLY: In the last minute a guy on the high track has fitted a gas tank, a fellow on the Engine Dress is putting in his second gear-box, the second of forty gear-boxes he'll put in during the next hour, three hundred and twenty the whole shift. That's supposed to be what an average man can do on an average shift.

LES: All agreed by negotiating committees, Walt, meeting with the management.

WALLY: What the hell is an average man? Or an average shift? Or an average time of day? Who feels the same at night as in the morning? Who feels the same after eight hours trying to keep up with the track? There's no average time, only Ford time.

LES: All the same that was a big step forward, getting those times established. Before, they could speed up the line whenever they wanted. We'd be doing thirty cars an hour, just coping, no time to spare, and suddenly we'd find we were falling behind. They'd changed the speed, we were doing thirty-five.

JAMES: Who was responsible?

LES: The production manager. Only way he could make more money was increasing output. Only way he could increase output was pushing more cars along.

WALLY: That's a growth economy, brother.

LES: They had a factory in Cologne. If we started getting too bolshie, they'd put us supervisors on what they called 'a course'. Which was to see how they did things in Cologne. But there was no Germans on the line down there—only Spanish and Turkish immigrants. Transients. They could

35

do thirty-five an hour and if they didn't they were sent back to their mud-huts.

WALLY: Which is what they call an economic miracle.

LES: All part of the rat-race.

WALLY: Same thing before the war in Detroit. Ford hired gangsters to beat us up. I swore then I'd never take promotion. What for, Les? A white coat, a clock, a cheque-book?

LES: What about the Cherokee? I'd never have got that as a line operative.

WALLY (*to* JAMES): Still working, the track. Never stops. (*Looking at watch.*) Since I last mentioned him, the fellow on the Engine Dress has fitted three more gear-boxes.

JAMES: Absolutely fascinating!
(*He liberally replenishes their glasses.*)

LES: You never been on the shop-floor, James?

JAMES: I fear not. An appalling omission.

LES: You'd find it wonderful in many ways.

JAMES: I must arrange to go.

LES: Nothing stops the line. If a man's hurt, the supervisor's top priority is filling the job. Only after that's done, you can see if the casualty needs to go to sick bay. Right, Wally?

WALLY: Right.

LES: And I think if the lads got faith in their supervisor, they see that's the best way. One night, I remember, just as a shift was starting, a fellow drops down right by the line. . . . 'Course, all the lads crowd round but just then the buzzer goes and the line starts moving. I said "All right, lads, get on with your work." And being as they trusted me, see, James, they turned to it, sticking on the hub-caps while I got an operative to take the casualty's place, then called the ambulance men. D'you know, he was stone dead. Gone off the first instant, they reckoned, and been laying there ever since. So—as I said to the lads during tea-break— no purpose would have been served by disrupting the line, losing bonuses. No, that line never stopped.

WALLY: Nor did the men. That's why I quit.

36

(NANCY *and* MAY *come from bus.*

  NANCY *has changed to something tweedy.*)

NANCY: It's been confirmed that the Scrubbers are the cause, James.

MAY: Dirty little animals.

NANCY: They should be thrown into gaol along with the trades-union leaders. Don't you agree, Mrs. Lorimer?

JAMES: Mother, you must learn to distinguish between a gang of unwashed narcissists and a body of democratically elected delegates. Mrs. Lorimer, a brandy and soda?

MAY: Gracious me! What with the Snowball earlier and all that wine over dinner, you'll have me squiffy.

JAMES: I do assure you, the claret could have only a benign effect.

WALLY: He means you're not as thunk as you drink you are.

MAY: No, thanks, really.

LES: Won't you sit down, Lady Rhyne?

NANCY: Thank you, I'm on my way to bed.

MAY: Now are you sure you'll be comfy in the car?

NANCY: I'm as tough as old nails. Hill-walking, climbing——

MAY: Only that, if you wanted to come in the Cherokee, we could easily kick out Wally.

NANCY: Most considerate, but absolutely not. Good-night. God bless you.

   (*They wish her good-night and she goes to estate car and rummages in boot for blankets.* EVELYN *comes from tent.*)

EVELYN: Smells like Christmas out here.

LES: I'm turning in. (*To* MAY.) You left that drop of water?

MAY: In the galley sink.

LES: 'Night, all.

   (*They say good-night and he goes into bus.*)

JAMES (*to* EVELYN): Evelyn, may I get you a nightcap?

EVELYN (*hand instinctively to her wig*): Pardon?

JAMES: A little brandy?

EVELYN: Gracious no! You'll give me heartburn.

   (NANCY *has found blankets in boot and shut it. She has also looked at nearside wheel and now comes down.*)

NANCY: James, I thought your friend said he'd replace our

37

wheel.

JAMES: In the morning, Mother.

NANCY: Well, I hope so. *You* can't do it.

JAMES: He needs the morning light.

NANCY: We want to make an early start.

JAMES: We must hope that's possible. Good-night, everyone.
Sleep well.

(*They go off together, left.*

A child cries, not far off. An adult's voice shouts. EVELYN
is sitting with WALLY *at the table, preparing her face for
sleep, by the light of the gazlamp.* WALLY *pauses in smoking
to look towards the cry.* MAY *wanders down to the fence and
stares over audience.*)

MAY: *By the shore of Gitche-Gumee*
By the shining big sea-water
Stood the wigwam of Nokomis
Daughter of the moon Nokomis—

WALLY (*joining in*): *Dark behind it rose the forest,*
Rose the black and gloomy pine-trees,
Rose the firs with cones upon them—
(*They stop, laughing silently.*)

EVELYN: That's cheerful.

MAY: Wally and I learnt that as kids, didn't we, love?

WALLY: We used to say it over and over—

MAY: I always say it when I'm frightened.

EVELYN: Are you frightened now?

MAY: Oh, no!

WALLY: When I first went out to Canada, I used to say it over
when I was all alone.

EVELYN: How could you stand it?

WALLY: What?

EVELYN: Being all alone like that?

WALLY: I wasn't alone that much. Not enough, in fact. Pretty
soon like everyone else I finished in the city. But I never
forgot those days. The extremes of hot and cold. Some night
maybe you've bivouacked under canvas in the Rockies.
And you leave your tent-flap open, 'cause in the foothills
it can stay pretty warm. But you'd be sorry! Halfway

38

through the night there'd be this god-awful stench so bad it would wake you up. And this breathing and snuffling right there in the tent—

EVELYN: Oh, Lord—

WALLY: You'd open your eyes and turn your head, real slow, so's not to notice and there he'd be. This durn great grizzly bear . . .

EVELYN: I should die of fright.

MAY: *This is the law of the Yukon,*
That only the strong shall thrive,
That surely the weak shall perish—
And only the fit survive.

(LES *appears at door with wet hands and face.*)

LES: Where's the flipping towel then? Eyes full of soap and water—

MAY: Wasn't it hanging on the bulkhead by the barometer?

LES: No, I felt there.

MAY: Can't you think where you last had it?

LES: I *haven't* had it.

MAY: Oh! Lie down and I'll breathe for you . . .

(*They go back into bus, arguing. Pause. Sounds of a party, drunken voices. Someone sings.*)

WALLY: Yessir, the wide open spaces, not a living soul for miles.

EVELYN: I should hate it. I like people. People are my life. When my husband Freddie was alive, he used to take me on these walks. Not a car in sight, just birds. I cried on one occasion. He said, "Sweetheart, what on earth's the matter?" I said, "It's all this country!" He said, "This is beautiful." I said, "It may be beautiful, but I can't stand it."

(*Song ends. Applause and cheers. Sounds of party breaking up.*)

Civilization's good enough for me. People. The dragshop. Dancing.

WALLY: You a dancer?

EVELYN: Latin and off-beat, yes. And you?

WALLY: At one time, in a sociable way, nothing serious.

EVELYN: I was only thinking perhaps that's why you never took the plunge—not being stuck on dancing? Sixty per cent of

39

the married couples in this country first bumped into each other on the dance floor.

WALLY: Sounds kinda clumsy.

(*She looks at him. He laughs helpfully. She laughs too.*)

EVELYN: You're pulling my leg. But really, I'm surprised you never felt the need of a partner.

WALLY: I was a rolling stone. A maverick. Besides as a young man I was awful shy.

EVELYN: You're the image of my late hubby. Shy. Suffered with his back. And to look at him on paper you'd have said he could no more dance than fly. But I think it's the challenge, the sense of achievement, the stimulus of other young couples all mad keen to win. You'd find yourself swept along in the mounting excitement of the championships. You must come and see my dresses. They fill two rooms. Together with Freddie's.

WALLY: He wore dresses?

(*She looks solemn and again he smiles.*)

EVELYN: I like a man with a sense of humour. No, his suits and shoes. What size shoe are you?

WALLY: Nine and a half.

EVELYN: The same as Freddie!

(*She has finished her toilet and stows the equipment, closes the mirror. WALLY's still smoking. Sounds of the crowd have died away. A dog barks. Someone shouts it to silence. An owl hoots.*)

WALLY: Hear that?

EVELYN: What?

WALLY: Listen!

(*The hoot again.*)

EVELYN (*scared*): What is it?

WALLY: Only an owl.

EVELYN: I should be so frightened if you weren't here.

WALLY (*putting his hand on hers on table*): I'll take care of you.

EVELYN: Freddie and you! *He* was all for the call of the wild.

WALLY: Don't you ever get to feel romantic?

EVELYN: On occasion.

WALLY: Sure you do.

EVELYN: I sometimes sit for hours, dreaming away, my head in the clouds.

WALLY: You gonna tell me what you dream about?

EVELYN: When I'm in that mood? Oh, acquiring property. I own the house, of course, Freddie's life policy saw to that, but I'm afraid the upkeep comes expensive. So, in my position, I'm obliged to go on taking paying guests. And being a woman alone I'm always afraid they're going to take advantage. I remember one morning when my hubby was alive, I turned round to him I said, "Darling, that new fellow in the top back—?" He said, "What about him?" I said, "I believe he's got a dog in there." He said, "Never!" I said, "Well, if he hasn't he's been making some very funny noises in the night." Well, Freddie said he'd ask later and he went off to business. Now this was a day we'd organized a buffet for one of the girls in our formation team. She was like you, lived all alone, so we assumed she'd appreciate the gesture. Well, as I say, I went to the larder to see how my trifle had set. And there it was, just where I'd left it on the shelf in my best cut-glass bowl but, among the cream piping and sponge and tangerines, curled up in the middle, was a dead hamster.

WALLY: Jesus.

EVELYN: He'd gorged himself until his insides burst.

WALLY: That's awful.

EVELYN: Well, it may not sound that much compared to your grizzly bear . . . but when you think of the size of my larder and the size of the Rocky Mountains . . .

WALLY: Sure.

(*The* SCALES *gave up the animal fair some time ago but we now hear them droning through "Lloyd George Knows My Father".*)

EVELYN: Your place in Vancouver, you own the freehold?

WALLY: No, I just got a ground-floor room in a boarding-house. It ain't much but it suits me fine.

EVELYN: And you live there all alone?

WALLY: All on my lonesome, yeah. 'Cept for Bruce.

EVELYN: Bruce?

WALLY: My airedale.

EVELYN: No ties, then, no connections?

WALLY: No strings to my affections. That's right.

EVELYN (*sings*): *Fancy free and free for anything fancy . . .*
(MAY *appears in door of bus.*)

MAY: Les says we're wasting the gas.

EVELYN: He would.

MAY (*coming to turn out lamp*): He's not too bad.

WALLY: I guess it's time to hit the sack.

SCALES: *Father knows Lloyd George . . .,* etc.

MAY (*fondly, looking towards them*): Ah, bless their little hearts.

EVELYN: I hope they're not going to keep that up all night.
(WALLY *puts out cigar and takes glasses. All go into bus,
closing the door behind them.*

*Pause. Distant sirens. The singing of "Lloyd George" falters
and finally ceases as* GRANT *comes on cautiously from right,
looks about. He signals and* TRACY *follows on.*)

TRACY (*singing quietly*): *Lloyd George knows my father . . .,* etc.
(*They both continue singing but she goes into the toilet tent,
zips up the front.* GRANT *remains on guard, conducting his
daughter offstage, signalling to her to sing up.*)

GRANT: *Father knows Lloyd George . . .*

SCENE THREE

*In darkness hear cockcrow, then later morning sounds—birdsong, gusts
of radio music, children's cries, etc. borne on breeze.*

*Lights up: bright early sunlight. People come across on the verge;
they look about guardedly. Others are seen moving on verge beyond
farther line of cars. The people on the verge unzip the front of the
toilet tent and look in. One makes to go in, then stops, turns and
shrugs to the others, pointing to inside of tent.*

MAY *comes from bus with the waste-paper spike. She looks at the
intruders pointedly.*

MAY: Can I help you?
(*They go off, the way they came. She zips up front of tent.*

A RACING WALKER *crosses the stage swiftly, on the verge,*
right to left, wearing track suit and running shoes. MAY *comes*
down to see him off as NANCY *comes from upstage left, with*
blankets. MAY *picks up litter.*)

Good-morning!

NANCY: Oh, good-morning!

MAY: Manage to sleep?

NANCY: Like a top. And you?

MAY: I'm used to Les's snoring, but, what with my brother and
Evelyn at it too, I was put in mind of a silver band.
(NANCY *stows blankets in boot, then locks it and comes down.*)

NANCY: It would seem like a bar of chocolate for breakfast
unless James finds something in the village.

MAY: When these jams happen, they usually plague the life out
of you with southern fried chicken.

NANCY: There wouldn't be any left by the time they got to us,
we're too far in.

MAY: Sit down at our table, do.

NANCY: Absolutely not—

MAY: And share what's left of our food.

NANCY: You've been most generous but I'm quite happy on
grass. When you can find any these days. Under the
litter.

MAY: Shocking mess!

NANCY: The malaise of Britain: too many people.

MAY: And more pouring in every day, every shade and
persuasion.

NANCY: They should have enforced emigration years ago. Got
rid of the slackers. And stopped more coming in, too.

MAY: You ought to see our local post office. All in there with
their turbans sending money home to God-knows-where.
I said to my husband, "Things are looking darker every
day." I'm not having you on that grass, you'll catch your
death with the dew . . . now come into the body of the
kirk.

NANCY: I'm extremely obliged.
(*Sits at table.* MAY *goes on clearing litter.*)

MAY: We can pool the food that's left. Share and share alike.

What there is. If we'd known this was going to be so
serious, we'd have been less wasteful yesterday. We could
have spread the day's food over.

NANCY: My dear, you're not to blame. Not alone. The modern
world is possessed by greed. Any idea of selflessness, fair
shares, working for the common weal, seems to have gone
by the board.

MAY: The more they get, the more they want.

NANCY: Time will come there'll be none left. And serve them
right. You and I remember, don't we?

MAY: The shortages? Yes. Les and I were married in forty-
seven. I got extra coupons for my dress.

NANCY (*takes out a packet of cigarettes*): Cigarette?

MAY: Are they menthol?

NANCY: Yes.

MAY: Well, thanks.

(*They light up.* MAY *remains standing, pauses in work.*)

NANCY: I never expected to advocate a return to Socialist
austerity but, largely by default, the Labour régime stumbled
early upon a simple principle: you can't give everyone
everything. For instance, everyone can't live in a castle.
There aren't enough to go round.

MAY: And even if there were it wouldn't do. No. A few people
should live in castles and the rest of us go and look at
them.

NANCY: When I was a gel, only well-off people expected cars.
Look what happens when you try to put the world on
wheels!

(*She gestures at their situation.*)

MAY: The happiest time for Les and me was our early years.
We didn't have much money but we did see life. If we
went in a coach we thought it was our birthday.

NANCY (*nodding*): Simple pleasures.

MAY: I've always enjoyed simple things: working in the dragshop, a nice mystery with tea and biscuits in the interval,
a day by the sea with our children. And now our
grandchildren. Searching for unpolluted rockpools.

NANCY: The English coast was quite enough for most people,

44

but now who goes there? The mentally handicapped, the senile. Every able-bodied person is off to Tunis for the afternoon.

MAY: We had good times, too, during the war. Real characters people were in those days. Phyllis Griffith, now, an absolute dragon. Died at the age of eighty, still in harness, lighting one cigarette from another. During the blitz she spent every minute in the toilet, no one else could get in, but soon as the all-clear went she was down in Aldgate looking at the corpses.

NANCY: That's why you'd love the Highlands.

MAY: Oh yes!

(*Pause.* MAY *resumes work.* NANCY *smokes.*)

NANCY: Life's still peaceful there, like it used to be during the war. People there don't expect much and they don't get much and they know their place and when I say to my son, "Why can't life be like that everywhere?" he says, "You can't interfere with people's freedom." But do they appreciate freedom?

MAY: No.

NANCY: What they lack is a sense of purpose, moral purpose. You give them a new Freeway, they just take it for granted. When I was a gel, we had wonderful times but we were expected to reciprocate: housing committees, prison visiting, breaking the National Strike . . .

MAY: The juniors in our dragshop, they hardly know they're born!

NANCY: You never tolerate mutinies, I'm sure?

MAY: Mutinies?

NANCY: I believe in calling a spade a spade, Mrs. Lorimer— others may call them strikes, I call them mutinies.

MAY: Oh, we don't strike, no—

NANCY: And your husband in his car factory, I'm sure he's no agitator?

MAY: Well, at one time he had some funny ideas but since they put him on the staff—

(*The* RACING WALKER *returns from left to right.* NANCY *pauses and watches him.*)

45

NANCY: Is there any sign of the traffic moving?

(*He gives one bark of laughter and continues off.*)

MAY: I'd better wake the sleeping beauties.

NANCY: May I use your lavatory tent?

MAY: You can't at the moment. My husband was first up and he's taken the bucket. . . .

(JAMES *returns from right, wearing tweedy clothes, carrying walking-stick. Other hand is clasped inside jacket. Seems upset.*)

JAMES: Good-morning, May.

MAY: Good-morning.

JAMES: Good-morning, Mother. I hope you slept well?

NANCY: Don't tell me you had no luck. We've nothing for breakfast.

MAY: You can share our dry toast and milkless tea.

JAMES: I rather think we should discuss this *sotto voce*. As you may well imagine, the situation's giving rise to an acute food shortage.

NANCY: How are things at the end of the line?

JAMES: I didn't get to the end of the line. Only as far as the first village. . . . Mrs. Lorimer, take these inside quickly—

(GRANT *enters, as before, right. Sees* JAMES *take out two cartons of milk.*)

GRANT: Good-morning. D'you get that milk in the village?

JAMES: Ahm—yes.

GRANT (*checking wallet*): I hope they accept credit cards. About a mile, isn't it?

JAMES: Nearer two.

GRANT: Four miles walk! Oh, well, the kids are starving, so——

JAMES: I fear you're too late. I had to wait in a queue of several hundred yards and was one of the last to be served.

TRACY (*coming on during this*): Last? Why?

JAMES: Their stocks were exhausted.

TRACY: Surely there'll be more deliveries?

JAMES: Hardly possible till the road's cleared.

GRANT: Can't they use the far lanes to get through?

JAMES: If you recall, the high street forms part of the one-way link-road. The village can only be approached from one

46

direction—and that direction is now jammed solid.

(*Moment's pause as everyone begins to realize how serious the situation has become.*)

MAY (*to* GRANT): *Too late, too late, shall be the cry,*
                           Arnold the ice-cream man's gone by.

TRACY: How am I supposed to manage? My little boy virtually *lives* on milk.

NANCY: Won't he take the breast? Or are you too vain?

TRACY: Sholto's five and a half.

NANCY: Didn't you bring any food with you?

GRANT: There's very little room in the Kamikaze and usually we're at my wife's mother's place in a couple of hours.

MAY: You have one of these.

TRACY: Oh, no, thank you, we couldn't make you——

MAY: We've got no kiddies with us. If I had my grandchildren here, I like to think I might get a helping hand.

GRANT: How much do I owe you?

JAMES: Please don't think of it.

NANCY: Take the other inside quickly, Mrs. Lorimer.

TRACY: Well, thanks very much.

GRANT: Any point trying the other way? The Freeway?

JAMES: I was told the queues there are two miles long.

TRACY: It's totally mad, don't you think so? I mean hark at those cows in the sheds down there!

GRANT: And woken up by those bloody hens at dawn and we can't get an egg for breakfast. Krishna!

(*They go, right.* MAY *has gone into bus with milk.*)

NANCY: Have they stopped people joining on the end?

JAMES: I put that question to an Autoguard who was setting up a membership booth in the village. He said no.

NANCY: Well, they must.

(*A helicopter passes from right to left. The battering sound and again the blowing of the grass.* NANCY *and* JAMES *look up to it. It recedes.*)

JAMES: The Seventeenth Gloucestershire Light Horse! My old regiment!

(LES *comes from upstage, left between other vehicles. He is carrying a chemical lavatory bucket, with the lid closed. He*

*watches helicopter go, comes on to verge and puts down
bucket. Wipes brow with handkerchief.*)

Good morning, Les.

LES: Morning, all.

JAMES: You should have waited. I'd have helped with that.

LES: Good job I didn't. Bad enough as it was finding a place to
empty it where the families were still asleep. Couple of
times they woke up while I was trying to do it. Got very
nasty.

(*Unzips front of tent and takes out plastic bottle of chemical.*)

I was pouring it over the fence, of course, on to the field
the other side but . . . understandable people not wanting
that outside their front door. Odourless, but still unsightly.

(*Pours chemical into bucket.*)

NANCY: It wasn't nearly full last night.

LES: And d'you know what? I reckon people have been availing
themselves in the hours of darkness.

JAMES: Do you really?

LES: People without facilities.

JAMES: That's intolerable.

LES: Can't blame them. Very awkward.

(*Puts bucket and bottle in tent, leaves flap open.*)

JAMES: We'll post a guard. I'll work out a duty roster.

LES: You reckon?

JAMES: Much as it goes against the grain, we can't have you
emptying that bucket every five minutes.

NANCY: No indeed! There are far more pressing jobs to be done.
Have you had a chance to look at our tyre yet?

LES: Not yet, no.

NANCY: That sort of thing.

(*She goes into tent, zips front.* MAY *comes from bus.* JAMES
has gone to open boot of his car and put in stick.
He rummages. MAY *brings on more rubbish to put in the
pedal-bin.*)

MAY: *Home is the sailor, home from the sea
And the hunter home from the hill.*
D'you manage, love?

LES: Just about. Like to wash my hands.

48

MAY: The pitcher's empty. Evelyn's used the last for tea. *And* she had to use the gas, there's no paper left for the Vesuvius.

LES: P'raps a drop in the kettle for me.

JAMES (*coming down with shotgun*): Les, I hope you won't consider this melodramatic but we may need to make a show of arms.

LES: Go on.

JAMES: A polite request may not cut much ice with people desperate for a pee. I'm remembering the ugly scene in the village hypermarket. Can you handle a gun?

LES: I don't know. Must be thirty years since I——

JAMES: No matter. A glimpse will almost certainly suffice.

MAY: What for?

LES (*bewildered*): Keep strangers out the toilet.

MAY (*uncertain*): Oh?

JAMES: I don't travel armed in the ordinary way. So happens this weapon's been with my gunsmith.
(EVELYN *comes from bus.*)

EVELYN: I found a tomato juice in the cocktail cabinet. You'd like it for breakfast, I expect?

LES: Long as you don't come whining to me later on when you want a Bloody Mary.

MAY: Have to make it a Virgin Mary.

EVELYN: The vodka's gone in any case . . .
(WALLY *comes from the road, up left.*)

WALLY: Hi. Good-morning.

JAMES: Good-morning.

LES: Where've you been? I thought you were still in the Land of Nod.

EVELYN: Been laying breakfast all round your bunk, curtains drawn and everything.

WALLY: Got up early. Been down in the meadow yonder, picking mushrooms and blackberries.
(*Shows two plastic bags of fruit.*)

JAMES: How extremely enterprising of you!

WALLY: May be a little squashed. Had to keep them outa sight, people are getting hungry.

49

MAY (*taking bags*): My clever old brother!

EVELYN: We're eating inside this morning.

LES: I bet there's a good few toadstools amongst them.

WALLY: D'you sleep tight, Evelyn?

EVELYN: Not too bad, considering the quiet . . .

(*Goes into bus, taking bags of food.*)

WALLY: Got a shotgun, James?

JAMES: I judged it might be prudent to mount a guard. Over the loo.

WALLY: Yeah?

(*Takes gun and looks at it, working the breech, etc. NANCY has come from the tent.*)

A NURSE *comes on, down left, the first person to appear on our side of the fence. She carries a red-cross satchel, wears traditional uniform but rubber boots on feet, looks tired, grubby, anxious, aged eighteen plus.*

Everyone looks at her, then as she turns towards left, they also turn to see what follows. Two STRETCHER-BEARERS *carry on a* YOUNG MAN *with cropped head and some face hair. He's covered mostly by blanket but some wounds can be seen.*

BEARERS *are Indian or North African.*)

NANCY (*at fence*): Casualties? Through here?

NURSE (*to* BEARERS): You all right? Have a rest.

NANCY: Why are you bringing casualties through here?

MAY: Would you like some tea?

NURSE: Thanks very much.

NANCY: Good girl, May. Tea, as quick as you can.

(MAY *goes into bus as* GRANT *and* TRACY *wander on from their car. Everyone tends to move down to the fence for a good view of the casualty. The* BEARERS *put him down and stretch.*)

Why aren't the casualties going by helicopter?

NURSE: They're for reporters and V.I.P.s.

JAMES: The Freeway itself then? The service tracks?

NURSE: Accident victims only.

(*She makes the casualty more comfortable. He is unconscious.*)

NANCY: Then who's this?

NURSE: A Scrubber.

(*General surprise, curiosity, some draw back.*)

50

JAMES: They're not firing on the Scrubbers?

NURSE: All they told us was this fellow was in a group that started taking off their clothes and walking out to embrace the guards and offering posies of wayside flowers. One of the patrolmen panicked and fired three times in self-defence.

NANCY: Where are you taking him?

NURSE: Cottage hospital, the end of the linkroad.

NANCY: A National Health hospital?

TRACY: Oh, no!

GRANT: Poor bastard!

NURSE: I'm only doing what I'm told.

NANCY: He must be taught a lesson.

TRACY: All the same . . .

JAMES: Is it a sizeable demonstration?

NURSE: I believe it's over. They're helping the police with their inquiries.

NANCY: High time.

LES: How many were there?

NURSE: A dozen or so.

LES: And managed to cause a hold-up over a hundred miles long. Anyone that does that deserves no mercy.

JAMES: This will put paid once and for all to the Scrubbers' case against the Freeway. Their Puritanical performances on television, together with some fashionable indecency, have won them a measure of popular support. But I have always maintained that if the electorate heard their argument, they would see that it demands self-sacrifice. And seeing that, they would reject it.

(MAY *comes from bus with cups on tray.*)

MAY: We're out of sugar, I'm afraid.

NURSE: Oh, thanks.

MAY (*aside, to* NANCY, *of* BEARERS): Things are looking dark over there. Where are you taking him?

NURSE: Hospital in the village.

MAY: Poor kid.

LES (*turning on her*): He brought all this hardship on innocent people . . . halted the Freeway . . . old-age pensioners without toilets . . . they're no better than the A-rabs.

TRACY: Pardon me, I thought their idea was to bring the community back to a sense of community. I'm not saying theirs is the right way but surely——

LES: What? Share and share alike? Lot of rubbish! Public transport? Going *where* people tell you *when* they tell you. Call that freedom?

JAMES: Ah, but, Les, you forget that, whereas you and I would defend that freedom to the last drop of blood, the Scrubbers and their followers——

NANCY: Come on, James, wholesale freedom won't wash. Not for all this lot! A little bit here and there, by all means, but we can't let people wallow in it.

MAY (*to* NURSE): So is it all over now?

NURSE: The demo? Yes.

MAY: We'll be moving then. None too soon.

NURSE: Shouldn't count on that. Come on, Abdul . . .

(*The* BEARERS *finish their tea and give cups back to* JAMES.)

JAMES: How d'you mean?

NURSE: There's a work to rule or something. Farther up the Freeway. Nice cup of tea, thanks very much.

LES: Work to rule? Who's working to rule? Who said?

NURSE: Some of the Autoguards were saying. I didn't listen, I was busy.

(NANCY *has taken a note from her purse and gives it to* NURSE.)

NANCY: You'll see he's well looked after, won't you? Given the least harmful treatment?

NURSE: He'll be all right.

(*They go.*)

MAY: I wonder if his mother knows where he is? Not a bad-looking boy! If only he'd come to his senses, grow his hair, get a nice job and a car . . .

JAMES: Mother, I marvel at your buying him preferential treatment.

NANCY: I deplore the Scrubbers' methods, but their message makes sense. They want a return to a hardier, simpler way of life.

JAMES: A profoundly reactionary movement——

NANCY: Whereas your blessed unions are obstructing the Freeway just as effectively and for what? Greed. A bigger slice of the cake.

LES: Now just a minute, ma'am. We don't know yet what's happening on the Freeway but whatever that may be I can't allow you to mention those perverts in the same breath as a properly constituted trades union.

JAMES: Hear, hear.

LES: I come from a Labour family—you'll forgive me speaking frankly, James?

JAMES: My dear Les, your loyal support for the Labour movement only renews my faith in the *status quo*. Everything in its proper place.

LES: My father was a Labour man and his father before him. They spent half their lives queuing up for the charity handout, licking the boss's B.T.M., you'll excuse my French? I wonder what the Scrubbers would think of walking if they'd had to march all the way from Jarrow to make themselves heard in London?

MAY: Your father never marched from Jarrow. Nor your grandpa.

LES: Who said they did?

MAY: They lived in East Ham.

LES: I know that.

MAY: They used to go up West on the Fifteen bus.

LES: I only said they were working men. And their first taste of freedom was when my old man got a secondhand Prefect. Middle-aged he was by then. Spent his life making cars for other people and now he had his own. That old banger was a magic carpet to my dad! But if you'd tried to tell him his son would one day own a centrally heated Motor Home he'd have told you to pull the other. I got my own grandstand for point-to-points!

(LES *displays his bus to the others: this is a Credo.*)

If we feel like an Elizabethan blow-out, with jousting as an optional extra, then it's up the Freeway to Castle Howard. Anyone wants a look at Africa, we poodle down through

France, ninety ninety-five, no sense pushing, over the Pyrenees, take in a bull-fight. Then by ferry to Tangiers, Marrakesh, Casablanca, nothing to it. Tea in the Sultan's Palace, use a bit of film on the beggar boys, get some movie-shots of May on a camel——

MAY: Never again!

LES: —have a peek at the belly-dancers.

MAY: And the countryside can be super too, if you had the time to look.

LES: We've parked the Cherokee in some five-star car-parks, no doubt about that.

MAY: Red Square, all the old women cleaning up with their dustettes. Milan Piazza's got the best facilities. The Wailing Wall in Jerusalem wasn't much to write home about.

LES: A real let-down.

MAY: But I think my favourite for atmosphere is Mozart's house with the Viennese waltzes on the speakers.

LES: And all without leaving home—because our home's there with us!

TRACY: Oh, come on, you talk about Morocco, *I* used to be a belly-dancer. Before my husband and I were married. *And* I worked the Moroccan circuit.

GRANT: Perhaps it was you they saw.

TRACY: Perhaps. You drove out in your Motor Home and I flew from Gatwick. Don't you see that's absurd?

GRANT: Tracy would gladly have danced for you at home—in Henley-on-Thamesway.

LES: Belly-dancing was all laid on in the Sultan's Palace. All included in the one price. Tour, belly-dancing, savoury tea.

TRACY: It's not that I'm one of those ecology nuts——

GRANT: That whole Environment thing has been so commercialized!

TRACY: —but I like to think there'll be some country left when Stephanie and Sholto grow up.

GRANT: Right!

JAMES (*heatedly*): Arnold of Rugby rejoiced at the coming of the railway age, because he saw in it the end of feudalism.

Perhaps he was premature. But the *car* is the most powerful democratic instrument yet conceived. More effective than good intentions, more eloquent than assemblies. You cannot tyrannize the man with a Motor Home!

NANCY: While you're so busy not tyrranizing people you don't seem to have noticed that the world's become one vast garage!

JAMES: The great cultures thrive, virtually unscathed. London is London still.

NANCY: Hyde Car Park, St. James's Car Park, Regent's——

JAMES: Hostages to fortune.

NANCY: Thamesway.

JAMES: As an open river the Thames had been obsolete for years.

NANCY: The Seine too, I suppose? I remember when you could walk along its banks.

JAMES: Les can drive his Cherokee into the very heart of Paris, park by the Louvre, saunter through Île Saint-Louis——

LES: Where the French fall down is in their toilets. Don't you think so, James?

JAMES (*to* NANCY): Freedom of choice is more than river banks! The people have chosen traffic jams. Freely.

LES: I say, where the French fall down is in their toilets.

JAMES: I've never seen them do that, no . . .

MAY: Oh, yes, all through France, plenty of well-kept war-graves, nice crispy leaves, but finding a decent toilet's another story.

TRACY: That's what I came to ask—if I could possibly use your tent? My legs have been crossed ever since those birds woke me up at dawn.

LES: You the people used it last night?

GRANT: Not the only ones. There was a constant to-and-fro. I was singing lullabies into the early hours so——

LES: Then I'm supposed to empty it?

TRACY: Just that being next-door neighbours——

MAY: That's all right, dear, you go on.

GRANT: Thank you. Thanks a lot.

(TRACY *crosses to tent, goes in, zips up.* GRANT *waits.* EVELYN *comes from Motor Home.*)

EVELYN: First sitting for breakfast. Mushrooms on toast, tomato juice——

LES: Keep your voice down, Evelyn.

(*She looks about nervously.* MAY *collects cups left by* NURSE. *Group breaks up.*)

EVELYN: I can take three of you.

MAY: My lady, you go in first.

NANCY (*moving towards door of bus*): Are you sure it's no inconvenience?

(*Follows* EVELYN *in.* WALLY *makes to follow.*)

LES: James, you first. Wally can wait.

JAMES: Quite out of the question.

LES: Then I'll wait with you.

JAMES: How kind.

LES: Leave us some, mind, Wally, I know you.

(WALLY *follows* MAY *into bus.* JAMES *and* LES *remain,* GRANT *going off right to his car.*)

The only hearty thing about him, his appetite.

JAMES: Les, may I say how inspiring it was to hear you defend our cherished way of life so warmly?

LES: I never meant to argue the point with Lady Rhyne, only——

JAMES: Please! Mother's extreme views sometimes cause her to lie down with some quite unsuitable bedfellows. Scrubbers, trendy-wendies, breast-beaters. How did Burke put it, d'you remember? Yes: it is a general popular error to imagine the loudest complainers for the public to be most anxious for its welfare.

LES: Fair enough.

JAMES: I'm happy to say the P.M. has never for a moment been taken in by their pleas for the simple life. What he rather quaintly calls The Golden Age Bit.

LES: Who's that?

JAMES: The Prime Minister.

LES: Ah.

JAMES: You've never met?

LES: He came round the works one day. Our paths crossed in

56

Paint, Trim and Assembly.

JAMES: What impression did you form?

LES: I didn't get all that close.

JAMES: Great shame because I'm sure that, despite your doctrinal differences, you'd find him a man after your own heart. And I shall certainly pass on to him your support for his policy of a car to every citizen.

LES: Fair enough.

JAMES: On Tuesday, in fact. He'll be at our game lodge for a few days' stalking. We're driving up to make it ready and my wife's arriving later by air. So if you find your ears burning, you'll know the name Les Lorimer is being bandied about over the port and Stilton. With your permission?

LES: That's all right.

JAMES: Much obliged.

LES: What sort of a fellow is he?

JAMES: Most agreeable.

LES: A lot of the lads on the floor reckon he's a bit lah-de-dah, you know, with his hunting, shooting and fishing.

JAMES: You may assure them that he hides an essentially forward-looking character behind a studiously antique manner. No Englishman would trust him otherwise. Look at the harm done to the government's image by that awful little shit, his cousin.

LES: Who?

JAMES: The Minister for Growth.

LES: Used to be a woman?

JAMES: That's him.

(TRACY *comes from tent and looks for* GRANT, *who comes from downstage of tent bringing children's plastic pot, which* TRACY *takes in. Suddenly a loudspeaker voice from behind the audience. Everyone onstage looks towards it.*)

VOICE: Attention, please, attention, all travellers. Under its present emergency powers, the Royal Freeways and Linkroads Authority has issued a movement order, the purpose of which is to restrict individual and collective mobility. Travellers may, by mutual agreement, enjoy the recreational facilities of those areas adjacent to their own on either side but longer journeys will be made only in emergencies, for which special passes will be required.

LES: What we going to eat if we can't go shopping?

VOICE: Voluntary services will be providing meals on wheels.
(TRACY *comes out.*
    LES *looks at* GRANT, *crosses to tent, zips up front.* TRACY *takes* GRANT's *arm and leads him off, up right.*)
Trespassers may be detained and questioned by armed rangers.

JAMES: This makes an armed guard imperative.

LES: People without facilities got to go somewhere.

VOICE: We hope for everyone's sake that the Wreckers' and Breakers' Union will accept the government's generous pay offer soon and help us get the Freeway moving again. Thank you.

LES: What's the unions got to do with it?

JAMES: Evidently some wage dispute's got stuck in the pipeline.
(COX *has come on from the right. Speaker's voice is heard repeating the message off left for another section of linkroad.*)

COX: Morning, all.

JAMES: Sergeant Cox, you can surely put us in the picture? How are the unions involved?

COX (*taking off cap, scratching head*): Lord above, I don't dabble in politics, my lord. I leave those to our friends in Whitehall.

LES: Last we heard it was the Scrubbers. What's the Wreckers got to do with it?

COX: I should like a word with Lord Rhyne, sir, if you wouldn't mind. (*Pointedly.*) In private.

LES (*taking hint, going into bus*): I'll see if breakfast's up yet.

JAMES: How very kind of you.
(COX *takes from his satchel a net bag containing oranges and chocolate. At the same time,* JAMES *takes out wallet and a letter. Food and a banknote change hands.*)
I'm extremely grateful.

COX: That's what we're here for, my lord.

JAMES: Could I put myself yet deeper in your debt by asking you to see this note's delivered?

COX: Leave it to me, sir.

JAMES: Glorious weather.

COX: Just what the gardens need.

(*Sound of sirens off left on Freeway.* COX *stows letter in satchel.* LES *looks out of bus.*)

LES: When you want it, James.

JAMES: Are you sure there's enough to spare?

LES: Fair shares for all.

(JAMES *goes in.* COX *looks at envelope.*)

COX: Downing Street?

(*Announcement continues off left.*)

VOICE: Attention, please, attention, all travellers. Under its present . . ., etc.

(*Loud outcry from offstage listeners.* COX *was moving across to left, about to continue along the road but the angry sound stops him.*

The noise breaks out again, with some bleating and a lot of yelling. This time it continues and turns into unison singing of "Why Are We Waiting?". COX, *without haste or any betrayal of indecision, turns about and makes off in the direction he came, right.*

Singing rises to climax and police whistles are blown as the lights fade.)

END OF ACT ONE

ACT TWO

Scene One

A news bulletin from House Speakers.

NEWSMAN: The Queen was at Greenwich today to welcome the
Amir of Kuwindi on his first state visit to the United
Kingdom. A report from our Royalty Correspondent.

WOMAN REPORTER: Many thousands of people added their
modern motley to the already resplendent panoply of this
right royal occasion. Not a few had spilled from office blocks
lining the north embankment of Thamesway, some were
tourists on a few days' safari in the capital and there was a
party of Kuwindi nationals whose traditional costume
contrasted gaily with the sombre Nagasaki knickers of the
crowd. The Amir arrived from Essex airport, an impressive
figure whose sudden bursts of uncontrollable laughter soon
won the hearts of the crowd and earned him the title Merry
Monarch. Her Majesty awaited him on the steps of Wren's
Naval College, beside it the rigging of *Cutty Sark* dwarfing
the brave outline of *Gipsy Moth*. And, behind, as the sun
shone at the bidding of the state trumpets, rose the dazzling
glitter of Greenwich Car Park. After exchanging greetings,
the two sovereigns went walkabout among a casual throng
of powerful merchant bankers. Then, almost as if by magic,
it seemed, the royal motorcade was off upstream to
Westminster and the Palace!

(*Lights up.*

Late evening. Moonlight.

EVELYN's *radio is on the table, beside a lighted gazlamp.*
The three families are standing downstage at the fence, each

holding a vessel of some kind, waiting, faces turned towards right. They span the whole width, left to right: JAMES, EVELYN, LES, MAY, NANCY, GRANT, WALLY and TRACY.

The side panel is open, as at end of Act One, revealing the kitchen.

Sound FX from speakers replace voice: cannon, fanfares, ceremonial.

From the right a water-tank on wheels is pulled by two WATERMEN, uniformed West Indians. They use two half-litre bottles to measure out water, one filling from tap, the other pouring into the waiting vessels. An F.O. spotlights their work.)

WATERMAN: Water! Get your water here!

(Pours TRACY's. She expects more.)

TRACY: That all?

WATERMAN: Half a litre each.

TRACY: And two children?

WATERMAN: Where? *(As she points.)* Another litre.

GRANT: How long's that supposed to last?

WATERMAN: Same time tomorrow night.

GRANT: Krishna!

(WATERMEN go on to WALLY.)

NANCY: That's impossible. I'm sure you could allow us more than that. I understand there must be rationing but——

WATERMAN: Half a litre each, lady. I don't make the rules, I'm only doing my job.

(GRANT and TRACY go off, right, to car. WALLY goes up to bus with his ration, leaves it, comes down again with another jug or pan and takes a new place between EVELYN and LES.)

(Pouring hers.) Any case you got a Motor Home. They carry a hundred litres. More.

NANCY: That's not ours. No, no.

(WATERMEN move on to MAY.)

MAY: No, that's ours, but it's less than a year old so it's not in working order yet.

LES: We only had a jerrican and that's all gone.

WATERMAN: Should have been more careful when you had it.

(NANCY has taken out purse and MAY takes her water to bus.)

61

NANCY: It's barely enough to wash one's hands.

WATERMAN: This is for drinking. There's people on the Freeway had none at all.

(WALLY *gets a second ration and goes up to pour it into the first. No one seems to notice.* NANCY *has found a banknote. The doling out continues.*)

NEWSMAN: Afterwards the Amir told reporters how surprised and dismayed he'd been to see so many empty parking spaces along the banks of Thamesway. He gave one of his roars of laughter and wondered whether Britain still deserved her position as a second-rate power if so few of her citizens could afford cars. Or petrol? He added, laughing even louder.

(*All have now been served. The men are going off, left.* JAMES, LES, EVELYN, MAY *and* WALLY *go to kitchen.*)

WATERMAN: Water! Get your water here!

NANCY: I say, look here! We'll make it worth your while . . .

(*They go off. She waves money and follows. In the kitchen there are furtive preparations.*

NANCY *returns, putting banknote back into her purse. She sits at the table.*

Radio crackles and we hear the distorted voice of the NEWSMAN. NANCY *turns up volume, but no use.*)

NEWSMAN: . . . Church leaders and TV stars have joined the government's plea to get the Freeway moving. In places of worship throughout the country . . .

(*Fades for good.* NANCY *shakes the radio then switches off.*)

NANCY: Too much! Really!

(*Others have come from bus and stand formally behind her.* MAY *and* EVELYN *carry plates,* JAMES *brings glasses on a tray and* WALLY *a glass jug.*)

MAY (*singing*): *Happy birthday to you—*

EVELYN, LES & WALLY: *Happy birthday to you—*

ALL: *Happy birthday, dear——*

JAMES (*as others falter*):—*Mother!*—

ALL: *Happy birthday to you!*

NANCY: How terribly kind. You really shouldn't have.

(*They put the plates on the table, on one a bar of chocolate, on the other some mandarins, broken into segments.*)

EVELYN: Don't thank us. Your son provided the food.

LES: Black market.

JAMES: I fear so, what little there is. But I couldn't allow your
birthday to pass without some ceremony, however humble.
Many happy returns, my dear.
(*He kisses her.*)

WALLY: Only got water to drink.

MAY: And none too much of that.
(*A glass is poured for each.*)

LES: That's where *my* little surprise comes in.
(*Shows small glass of red liquid.*)
The very last drop of Cherry Heering.

NANCY: For me? I simply couldn't.

MAY: No arguing now.

NANCY: Most kind.

LES: James ought to propose the toast.

JAMES: Indeed. As a political animal, I am bound to observe
Robert Frost's precept that—ahm—a diplomat is a man
who always remembers a woman's birthday but never her
age. So—sincere congratulations, Mother, and may your
future celebrations be in rather more agreeable surroundings.
Many happy returns!

ALL: Lady Rhyne, many happy returns, etc.

NANCY (*touched*): Dear friends . . . more agreeable circumstances,
yes, perhaps, but surely not more pleasant company.

JAMES: Hear, hear.

NANCY: Or more generous. I sometimes look at our countrymen
today, the spoon-fed young, the factory workers living on
the fat of the land, the dreadful people they put on
television with their awful voices, and I wonder if all sense
of obligation has quite gone with the wind. But meeting
you has reminded me of the essential decency of the
British, their love of the old ways. The old order changeth
certainly but in such a fashion that here in England at
least it never quite yields place to new. We are still in our
places, all of us, despite the efforts of trade unions, TV
communists——

63

JAMES (*firmly*): Mother, will you break the chocolate or shall I?

NANCY: Oh, yes, I will. You'd crumble or melt it.

JAMES: May has already divided the mandarins.

> (*Watched hungrily,* NANCY *breaks the bar into squares. Church bells are borne on the wind.*)

That can't be Evensong surely, it's far too late?

NANCY: Apparently the clergy are leading urgent prayers for the mutiny to be put down.

EVELYN: Gracious! Sunday! We should be back at business tomorrow.

> (*Hear off, right,* TRACY *and* GRANT *pacifying a child with another song.*)

SCALES: *When we are married we'll have sausages for tea,*

> *Sausages for tea—sausages for tea—sausages for tea——*
> (*Child cries louder.*)

TRACY (*off*): All right, love, we won't sing that one. "What shall we do with the drunken sailor?"—

> (*As they sing it,* MAY *turns back.*)

MAY: Poor kiddies are hungry.

> (*Quickly, almost furtively, they swallow their oranges and chocolate.*
>
> *Women sitting at table, men standing round. A searchlight sweeps across, settles on them for a moment, they squint into it, it moves on.*)

Why do they keep doing that?

LES: Some of the men with young kiddies, they're ganging up, roving about, breaking the movement order, taking food by force——

EVELYN: Oh, my lord!

WALLY: Don't you worry your pretty little head. We'll take care of you.

JAMES: You're well protected, Evelyn, I assure you.

WALLY: James's got a gun.

EVELYN: I can't stand bangs.

LES: You haven't touched your Cherry Heering.

NANCY (*sipping it, smiling*): Delicious.

LES: Too sweet for me, but I know the ladies like it.

> (*Bells again.*)

WALLY: I seen that church when I was down the valley . . . real olde worlde with a country churchyard . . .

JAMES: I should have joined them in prayer had it not been forbidden to climb the——
(*Gazlamp flickers. They all look at it while bells give way to other sounds—sirens, a speaker, a scream.*)

EVELYN: What's that?

WALLY: Kids playing. Hey, didn't a little bird tell me it's Evelyn's birthday this week too?
(EVELYN *laughs excitedly.*)
And how many candles will be on your cake?

JAMES: Wally, I appeal to you to remember Robert Frost.

EVELYN: I don't mind telling. Twenty-one!
(MAY *laughs and sings.*)

MAY: *She's got the key of the door*
Never been twenty-one before—

EVELYN: That's better. A song to cheer us up.

MAY: Music hath charms to soothe the savage breast.

EVELYN: Let's find some. We can dance as well. Who'll be my partner? Can anyone tango?
(*Switches on radio but no sound comes.*)

NANCY: The wireless is finished. Kaput.

LES (*turning it up in vain*): Shouldn't have wasted all the juice on ballroom music.

EVELYN (*hotly*): It's my portable! Dancing is my life! Are you telling me how to use my own things?

LES: Steady, steady, simmer down——

EVELYN: If you had your way it would be news, news, news, party politics. How we're falling behind the rest of Europe and must get bigger lorries to catch up and the Lord knows what! Where's the fun in that?

LES: Don't bite my head off—blimey O'Riley!

EVELYN: People want something cheerful, to take you out of yourself, so we can't hear those blessed bells, they're enough to drive you cracked.

NANCY: Pull yourself together, young woman.

MAY (*comforting*): There, there, love—

EVELYN: I don't know which is worse, the quiet or the bells and

65

screams—

LES: If people are going to lose their sense of humour——

EVELYN: What's funny about it? Look at us all! What is there to laugh at?

(*Cries. Others try to pacify her.*)

MAY: Never mind, love—worse things happen at sea.

(WALLY *suddenly sings.*)

WALLY: *Last night you slept in a goose-feather bed*
 With the sheet turned down so bravely oh,
 But tonight you will sleep in a cold open field
 Along with the raggle-taggle gipsies oh—

MAY: That's not very cheerful. Give us one of your army songs, Wally.

LES: Keep it clean. Mixed company.

WALLY: Give you one about the navy, one you can all join in. You join in, Evelyn?

(*She nods bravely.* WALLY *stands apart and sings.*)

 Sons of the sea—
 Bobbing up and down like this—

(*Each time he sings this he bounces on his feet.*)

 Sailing every ocean—
 Bobbing up and down like this—

(*Sings it through, replacing every other line with this phrase and bouncing to it. The others gradually join in, as he bids them. Even* JAMES *and* NANCY *find themselves bouncing the second time round until the spotlight sweeps across and finds them. They stop ridiculously as it lingers on them. The light goes on.*)

EVELYN: I'm not sitting down again, not now I'm on my feet. Isn't someone going to ask me to dance?

LES: Better make it the last waltz.

WALLY: Maybe I can manage that.

(MAY *sings a popular waltz.* WALLY *bows to* EVELYN *and they start dancing. Other voices join* MAY's *and* JAMES *crosses and invites her.* WALLY *falters.*)

Pardon me.

EVELYN: Oh, no, you're a natural. On a sprung floor in Freddie's pumps, you'd soon get the feel.

(*Sings with others for some moments.* MAY, NANCY *and* LES
*provide music but other neighbours drift in from surrounding
vehicles, including* GRANT *and* TRACY. *They join the singing,
perhaps dance.* EVELYN *begins to imitate a TV Presenter.*)
When she's not dancing, Evelyn's in the wig department
of a large dragshop. Wally hails from British Columbia and
used to be with the C.P.R.
(*The gazlamp splutters and goes out. Completely dark.
Singing dies away. Dance stops.*)
Oh, no!

LES: That's the end of that.

MAY: Put the kitchen light on.

LES: Run the batteries down? Economy's even more essential
now——

WALLY: Who cares? It's fine in the moonlight. Don't you think
so? (*Sings.*) *By the light of the silvery moon*—
(*People join in again and the dancing resumes. They have
hardly started when there is a sound of amplified tubular bells
from speakers behind the audience.*)

VOICE (*speakers*): Attention, please! That signal is the curfew.
(*Groans and a few sheep bleats. Voice continues over.*)
Travellers should now return to their vehicles and when
the sound is heard again, it will be the signal for Lights
Out.
(*The party breaks up with some complaining. The furniture is
folded and stowed by* LES, WALLY *and* JAMES. GRANT *gets
sleeping bag from bonnet-boot of his sports car, then goes off.
Women clear food utensils.*)
The grass verge should be cleared of furniture. The
Linkroads Authority will not be responsible for loss or
damage. Groups of transient workers are known to be
plundering up and down the Freeway, so please ensure that
doors and windows are fully secured.

EVELYN: Lord above! I said at the time they should never have
let them in the country. They're so hard to see in the dark.
(JAMES *goes to boot of car, where* NANCY *is already looking for
nightclothes.* EVELYN *and* MAY *go into bus.*)

VOICE: Reveille will be at six hundred hours. Inflammable

67

material such as paper and plastic will be burnt before seven hundred. Immediate disposal of perishables will be delayed due to a work-to-rule in sympathy with the Wreckers' Union.

NANCY: That settles it! We *must* have martial law.

JAMES: Please, Mother——

NANCY: The alternative is epidemic! Which d'you want?

(*Angrily goes into bus, closing door. JAMES loads shell into his gun. The three men assemble, centre.*)

JAMES: Two rounds each, I believe you follow me, Les.

LES: Yes and Wally's last. The car open?

JAMES: Yes. I'll wake you at one. Good-night.

(*They say good-night and go off, up left. JAMES patrols the area.*)

VOICE (*speakers*): It is strictly forbidden to feed Alsatians patrolling the perimeter fence. Animal-lovers are reminded that guard-dogs are trained to appear hungry. Keep your distance and do not—repeat not—allow children to pat their muzzles. I am empowered by the Royal Freeway Authority to wish you pleasant dreams.

(*The curfew signal is repeated and dies away. The announcement is repeated at a distance. Spotlight flashes across and JAMES dodges behind the toilet tent, unseen. The spotlight examines the area then moves on.*

Man's voice raised in anger, siren on Freeway, last phrase of church bells from the village. JAMES comes from hiding as the light goes. TRACY and GRANT begin wearily singing "Old MacDonald Had a Farm" and JAMES goes into tent. The barrel of his gun protrudes between the flaps.

Lights out.)

SCENE TWO

During the blackout, sound of animals and cockcrow. Then the cry of a woman in labour. Then two shots, some way off. Angry dog barks.

Light up on empty stage: a dull, cold light without shadows, and as the scene proceeds, it becomes more clouded.

68

LES *comes from up left, obviously from sleep.* JAMES *follows, un-rolling shirt-sleeves.*

JAMES: Those shots sounded close.

LES: No sign of Wally.
   (*They approach the tent.*)
   Wally! You in there?
   (WALLY *comes stealthily from up right, far side of road, carrying rifle and more food slung over shoulder in net bag. He looks an accustomed hunter.*)

JAMES: Sleeping, d'you think?
   (LES *unzips tent.* WALLY *approaches from behind, watching with interest. Raises gun to shoulder.*)

WALLY: Get your arse outa there! That's a private toilet.
   (*They turn. He pulls trigger but it's not loaded.*)

LES: Where've you been?

WALLY: Village over the hill.
   (*Brings dead pigeon from jacket.*)
   Had to use both shells. I'm a little rusty.

JAMES: Well done!

LES: You left the tepee unattended.

WALLY: Come on Les. They're doing that in the open.

LES: We're not.

WALLY: Might as well. Being the only ones with a toilet is kind of silly, don't you think? James, what do you say? If nobody has any toilets, what have we got to lose?

JAMES: Nothing but our chains?
   (WALLY *and* JAMES *laugh together.*)

LES (*resentfully*): Your idea is to mount a guard.

JAMES: Situations alter. I rather incline to Wally's pragmatical approach.
   (*Takes gun from* WALLY.)
   Certainly the first time this has been used for poaching.

WALLY: Nearly had to shoot a guard-dog but he lost my scent.

JAMES: You shouldn't take such risks.

WALLY: The other side there ain't so many patrols. Ground's too rough. No crops. Not many rangers. This is from the village church.

(Shows contents of bag: vegetables, bread, fruit.)

JAMES: A Harvest Festival, I imagine.

LES: Stealing from a church? Blimey O'Riley!

JAMES: Such offerings go to the needy of the parish. I rather think we might qualify.

WALLY: Say grace over it.

LES: Don't know if they can pluck this bird. Looks like we're in for some rain at last.

(Goes with food into bus. WALLY and JAMES go up left, WALLY to exit, JAMES to open boot and put in gun. NANCY comes from left, goes to door of bus, shouts in. Now wearing trousers.)

NANCY: Come along, you gels, there's work to do. Bring blankets and all your water to the pink Pegasus six cars up. Don't hang about. Young woman with a poor sense of occasion has gone into labour. Even the voluntary ambulanc brigades have mutinied now so she's going to need all the help we can give her.

JAMES: Good-morning, Mother. I'd no idea you were up.

NANCY: Didn't you hear those cries?

JAMES: Cries?

NANCY: Fine guards you make.

JAMES: Anything I can do?

NANCY: You! Good God!

(Gives bark of laughter and goes. He comes down, considering this as PAYNE enters from up left.)

PAYNE: Morning, my lord. Just came ahead to make sure you're here. Anyone else about, sir?

(Brusquely searches area.)

JAMES: They're in the Cherokee and at the car—why?

(PAYNE signals to COX who has come on upstage. He signals off and several camouflaged troopers come on with small arms, checking out ground, etc., followed by plainclothes security man with walkie-talkie. He shuts door of bus, posts troopers, signals to COX, who signals off.)

PAYNE: Visitor for you, sir. The Minister of Movement.

(BARRY enters by road, with photographer; fifty, ruddy face, much of it hidden by joke moustache, a suburban squire in tweedy checks, carrying shooting-stick.)

JAMES: Barry!

BARRY: James! I couldn't believe you were really stuck in this bloody shambles! The Prime Minister couldn't believe it either, and, as he knew I was coming to do a traditional walkabout, he asked me to find you.

JAMES: A most agreeable surprise. However, my note was only to explain that Mother and I shan't be at Glencromarty to welcome him. The staff expect him and he knows my ghillie from my father's days so——

BARRY: Where *is* Nancy?

JAMES: Delivering a baby.

BARRY: She doesn't change.

JAMES: That would be against her principles.

(BARRY *moves down to fence and breathes deeply*.)

BARRY: Aah! That's better.

JAMES: One of your company's superphosphates.

BARRY: You ought to smell the Freeway!

JAMES: Is it bad?

BARRY: Three lanes of traffic jammed solid for eighty miles? For three days and nights? You wouldn't chuckle it's bad. I was longing to get away from Town and the Amir of Kuwindi's bean feast but when I got a whiff of that—!

JAMES: I haven't seen him for years. Since school, in fact.

BARRY: I might have guessed you'd know him.

JAMES: He fagged for me. Always wanting to be beaten. Nasty little turd.

BARRY: No change there, except he's grown a bit. But the Freeway was one worse.

JAMES: I'm glad you've seen for yourself. Now perhaps you'll get things moving.

BARRY: Any suggestions how?

JAMES: Surely a wage settlement with the Wreckers' Union? Get Bill Brewer to rally the moderates for a show of strength with the extremists. A swift return to work, open the bottlenecks, get the traffic moving.

BARRY: Of course, you've had no private information. New experience for you, knowing only what the public knows. The chief blame lies with your friend Willie in Housing.

Weren't you at Eton with him too?

JAMES: Oxford.

BARRY: Those bottlenecks at the northern exits could only be cleared by wholesale demolition. All those market crosses and railway bridges kept up by crackpot preservationists, they'd have been easy. But the main obstacles aren't village pumps, they're post-war housing estates, geriatric homes, obsolete blocks of flats. You can't knock them down because of the people living there. Now this prize duffer Willie made such a cock-up of the housing programme there isn't anywhere to move them all. We can knock down a few Wesleyan chapels to show our heart's in the right place but that's not going to clear this lot! Which is the real issue, d'you agree, to get the Freeway moving?

JAMES: Absolutely. The Freeway's more than a road, it's an article of faith.

BARRY: There you are.

JAMES: The only single issue on which all parties are prepared to sacrifice every principle.

BARRY: Which is why we must be grateful to the Wreckers' and Breakers' Union. A jam like this could bring down the government, if there wasn't someone standing by to hold the country to ransom.

JAMES: You mean—act as scapegoat for the government?

BARRY: They'll get a whacking great wage increase.

JAMES: Sincere unionists would call that a bribe. I would myself.

(*Pause.* BARRY *moves upstage a few steps, opens shooting-stick, sits.*)

BARRY: James, I've never spoken out to you before. At your dinner-table and mine I've always had too much to learn from you about how the country's run and the people who run it. As a boy you rode piggy-back on Prime Ministers, kings blacked your boots at school. You're among the kindest, most civilized men I know. You're gifted with all the qualities one learns to value most highly: indiscriminate courtesy, unassuming confidence, unflinching patriotism, love of liberty, a total lack of regard for personal gain——

72

JAMES (*who has been trying to interrupt*): I simply cannot allow you to continue——

BARRY (*continuing forcibly*): Qualities bred by an almost invisible structure of privilege and sustained by an absence of responsibility. You love the Common People because you know fuck-all about them. At fourteen I left the elementary school and went as a tea-boy to the light engineering works.

JAMES: Most vividly described in your memoirs, yes.

BARRY: Don't turn this into a mutual admiration contest.

JAMES: Was I doing that?

BARRY: I only mention my early years to show you that I know the People at first hand. I was *one* of them. And my political life is devoted to improving the People's lot while making sure they never actually gain control. We daren't let them. And most of them don't want to. They want a bigger slice of the cake, not the bakery. The bright ones amongst them, like me, get out sharpish. And down on the floor you're left with a few militants, nasty little Hitlers, and the Men, the Majority. That's what it comes down to, James. Natural inequality.

JAMES: I prefer to say difference, variety.

BARRY: All right. There are two fundamentally "different" kinds of people—Us, the ones in charge, and Them, the ones who clear the shit away. Now I'll do all I can to see they get decently paid for doing it but I'll make bloody sure they're not allowed any real say. So don't tell me we're bribing the unions . . .

(*A disturbance at the left. They turn to see a* GUARD *struggling with* NANCY.)

NANCY: Take your hands off me! Where's your officer?

COX: Let the lady pass, that man.

BARRY: Sorry, Nancy, I'll have that bloke on a fizzer.

JAMES: You remember Barry Potter, Mother?

NANCY: You caught in this jam as well?

BARRY: I'm on a walkabout. Since the last reshuffle I'm Minister of Movement.

NANCY: Time they shuffled again.

BARRY: I do apologise. But take what you need from the car and

I'll lift you off.

NANCY: I'm not leaving now. This young woman's four fingers dilated. Where are my helping girls?

(MAY *and* EVELYN *bang on door of bus.* NANCY *goes to it.*)

Let them out this instant.

(BARRY *nods to* GUARD *and he opens door.* MAY, EVELYN *and* LES *come out, the women with blankets,* LES *with kettle. They start explaining.*)

No excuses now. If we don't look sharp, she'll manage this birth without us.

(*Leads off, left, others following.* BARRY *smiles, then makes to go.*)

BARRY: You'll persuade her to be ready in about ten to fifteen minutes?

JAMES: Most kind of you but we'd rather stay.

BARRY: I've got my orders. The Prime Minister told me——

JAMES: Then I must beg you to make our excuses. These people have become our friends—wage-slaves or not.

BARRY: Fact is, they'll all be leaving soon. By Shanks's Pony. I've already recorded an announcement. They'll be playing it as soon as we're airborne.

JAMES: This multitude by foot? Why?

BARRY: The welfare services aren't up to it. Jesus wept, you know what shape they're in. They can barely cope with the handicapped, the geriatric, people without cars, that class of person. But we've got the population of a sizeable town out here! With no plumbing!

JAMES: None of this affects our intention to stand by our friends. You may describe them as shit carriers, you may use the advantage of your lowly birth to denigrate their intelligence but——

BARRY: My dear fellow, I've enough problems——

(LES *comes from left, goes into tent and brings out bucket, with lid closed.*)

So much easier for us all if you collect your essential baggage and come with me. When the Freeway's cleared, an Autoguard will drive your car up to Glencromarty—

JAMES (*leading him to* LES): I don't believe you know each other.

74

Barry Potter, Les Lorimer.

(LES *puts down bucket, wipes hand on trousers, shakes with* BARRY.)

BARRY: How are you?

LES: Bearing up.

BARRY: Jolly good. That's the spirit.

LES: I know your face. You're—what's his name—?

JAMES: The Minister of Movement.

LES: That's him. Seen you often on TV. Seen you pop your head round the screen. Tally-ho!

BARRY (*wiping hand on handkerchief*): Keeping up the good work, I see?

LES: Someone's got to do it.

BARRY (*smiling at* JAMES): Exactly.

LES: Though my view is they ought to settle the dustmen's pay-claim or we shall have a sanitary problem.

BARRY: Then after that the Wreckers' hyper-claim and after that Charley Farnes-Barnes's hyper-claim and Uncle Tom Cobley-and-all's hyper-claim. That's the slippery slope, don't you think so?

LES: I couldn't agree with that altogether, not as a lifelong union man.

BARRY: It's your friends the unions that caused this bleeding shambles!

LES: I thought the Scrubbers had.

JAMES: Well said, Les.

BARRY: In the first place, yes, but now the Wreckers are taking advantage.

JAMES: But if the accident has been cleared, why can't we at least move northward as far as the bottlenecks?

BARRY: No point in that. At the London end there are massive queues of sightseers all coming up to look at the jam.

JAMES: Can't the police divert them, turn them back?

BARRY: Close the Freeway? Jesus wept!

LES: You can't do that, James.

JAMES: Stupid of me.

LES: We ought to start squeezing through the existing roads.

BARRY: Imagine it. Those Czechoslovakian juggernauts queueing in village streets, knocking prams over as they try to avoid the cathedrals! Pictures of carnage in the popular press! I'm not having that blood on *my* hands.

LES: Don't you worry. We've been through worse than this. Like Jerry found in the last lot, we can take it.

BARRY: Bang on!

JAMES: So you can assure us there's no question of evacuation?

BARRY (*annoyed*): We may have to act firmly but fairly to contain the danger to public health——

LES: Evacuation? How d'you mean? Reverse all the way back to the start of the linkroads?

BARRY: Reverse? Well——

LES: We'd never manage that, not with new people joining the queue every minute—

BARRY: Nothing of that sort, no.

JAMES: How would you feel about leaving the vehicles, Les?

LES: You're not going to try that? Blimey O'Riley, they'd skin you alive.

BARRY: Well, look, I mustn't keep you from your chores.
(*Makes to go but* JAMES *detains him.*)

JAMES: Skin you alive, you said, Les? Please enlarge.

LES: What was your election pledge? A car for every family and enough roads to drive them on? Not that I voted for you.

BARRY: Haven't we fulfilled that promise? We've crammed the streets with vehicles and covered the country with streets. All other public expenditure was cut back, truncated limbs of the social services were allowed to wither away—

LES: Granted. But one Scrubber demo, one justifiable wage dispute, and look at us! A single Freeway's not enough. There's got to be a whole interconnecting complex.

BARRY: Well, I shan't get them started nattering to you, enjoyable though it may be——
(*Moves away*, JAMES *follows.* LES *picks up bucket and moves towards left with it.*)

JAMES: Listen well to him, Barry. *Vox populi vox dei.* Or, as Burke put it, the temper of the people amongst whom he presides ought to be the first study of a statesman.

BARRY: Leave the people to me, James, you hold on to your

ideals——

(*Suddenly a recording of* BARRY's *voice from behind audience.*)

BARRY (*speakers*): Tally-ho, all freewheelers! This is the Minister of Movement, fresh from a traditional walkabout.

BARRY (*coming to fence*): Not yet!

JAMES: Oh, Lord!

(LES *stands listening.*)

BARRY (*speakers*): Now I've had a chance to see for myself the sacrifices you're making to help us deal with the crisis. A crisis brought about by two very different groups of extremists.

BARRY (*over this, moving to* SECURITY MAN): Get through and tell them to turn that fucking thing off——

BARRY (*speakers*): And I know from what you've said to me that when someone waves the big stick, you don't want us to wave the white flag.

BARRY (*back to fence*): I'll have that man on a charge so fast his feet won't touch the ground.

BARRY (*speakers*): And when I tell you that in the interests of public health we must now begin to evacuate the Freeway, I'm sure you'll accept——

LES (*same time*): What's that he's saying?

BARRY (*speakers*): —that it's one of those irksome things that sometimes have to be done.

BARRY: Potter here, are you receiving me? Over.

BARRY (*speakers*): Operation Dunkirk will begin immediately with Phase One: Leaving the linkroads. I can't promise that the Long Walk ahead will be without its hazards.

LES: Long Walk?

BARRY (*speakers*): But as you leave your keys in the vehicles and gather your essential hand baggage, you will know that——

(*Suddenly cut off.* BARRY *comes down to fence and stares over at speakers.*)

BARRY: I'll throw the book at that dopey bugger!

(*Neighbours have gathered on the road, attracted by the tannoy. From them and from offstage we hear rebellious noises.*)

LES: What's this about leaving our keys?

BARRY: As soon as the Freeway's clear, teams of Autoguards will drive the vehicles to some suitable car-park—say the Yorkshire Moors—and you chaps will be notified when you can go and collect——

LES: That may take months.

BARRY: I trust not.

LES: Months without a car! We're better off here.

BARRY: People are dying on the Freeway!

LES: People are always dying on the Freeway. That's part of the price.

MAY (*coming on from right*): Listen!

(*In silence hear a baby's cry.*)

He's a whopper. We reckon about four kilos.

JAMES: You see, Barry? People are being born as well.

MAY: I'm after some paper to make a parcel of the afterbirth.

LES: No paper left. All burnt. D'you hear that announcement?

MAY: What's it mean?

LES: They want us to leave our cars, start walking.

MAY: Who's they?

LES: Well, you know who this is, I expect?

MAY (*recognizing* BARRY): Looks like Tally-ho.

LES: It *is*.

MAY: My daughter likes you. She says you speak your mind.

BARRY: I try to.

MAY: She reckons anyone that's as rude as you are on TV must be telling the truth.

BARRY: Oh, that's marvellous! Isn't that marvellous?

MAY: Well, tell me, how are we going to live without the Cherokee? How shall I get to the corner shop the far side of the motorway with the nearest bridge a mile off? If I want a bag of sugar or a dozen eggs, Les takes me on the flyover, drops me by the shop——

LES: There's nowhere to pull in, so I keep circling the roundabout while she's in the shop till I see her waiting at the kerb.

MAY: He slows down to let me jump on, we're home again in no time. I often fetch the groceries for neighbours who can't get out—widows without cars, pensioners—they daren't go out, a lot of them, not now the pavements are so narrow.

LES: What are *they* to do?

BARRY: You'll have it back in a few weeks' time.

LES: In what condition? How do we know a lot of scruffs and gippoes aren't going to get inside?

MAY: An Englishman's Motor Home is his castle.

EVELYN (*coming from left*): May, Lady Rhyne says not to bother. The father's going to bury the placenta on the verge.

MAY: Love, they want us to leave the Cherokee and walk back to London.

EVELYN: I heard. I turned round straightaway. I said, "How am I to get to the Palais?" Now Freddie's gone I've no regular partner but I never miss a comp.

BARRY: A what?

MAY: A dancing competition. We pick her up.

EVELYN: With the one-way traffic non-stop round our crescent day and night the only other escape's by Underground. Well, picture me in a lurex bodice on the Bakerloo.

BARRY: It's appalling—and I speak for all parties when I say we're appalled at the hardship these dirty little scruffs are prepared to inflict on the people of Britain. And speaking for myself, if *I* ever meet a Scrubber up a dark alley, I'll have his guts for garters.

LES: What I'd like to ask is: your party's last election platform? Was it or was it not entirely based on keeping the Freeway moving?

BARRY: Like those of all other parties, yes.

LES: Well, we the car-makers played our part. The cars are still rolling off the line this very minute.

CROWD: Car workers? They can't grumble. Wish I could afford a Motor Home. They're only after what they can get (*etc.*).

MAY (*rounding on them*): You don't know what it's like on that assembly line. He used to come home, sit in the chair and go out like a light. When he was awake, it was more like sleep-walking. Months on end we hardly spoke to each other. The kiddies only saw him weekends and then his nerves were so bad he couldn't stand the sight of them. We weren't properly man and wife.

79

VOICES: Nobody forced them. It's a free country.

MAY: Well, it wasn't free when we were young. You worked where you were born and lucky to get it. And the day they took him off the line and gave him a white coat, we started living a decent life for the first time.

LES (*gently*): Well, that's all in the past now, love.

MAY: For you, but some poor devils are at it still.

LES: All transients though. No white European has worked on the line for nearly ten years. That was a big step forward for the British working man.

BARRY: Absolutely.

TRACY: Don't let's get into politics. If walking's the only way to get my children something to eat . . . d'you know what they had for breakfast? Playdoh.

(*Crowd murmurs sympathetically.*)

GRANT: Right! Modelling clay!

BARRY: Now that's victimization, *if* you like. And on the main roads it's even worse.

MAY: And they've got farther to walk.

LES: Pay the Wreckers what they want and we can all drive home—

CROWD: They ought to be strung up! Put them up against a wall (*etc.*).

BARRY: Now, come on, ladies and gentlemen, this isn't Russia! Not yet! Nor is it some airy-fairy Utopia. This is what you voted for. It's what you want. It's what *I* want. A free-for-all.

MAY: Free for who exactly? Not us. We paid for every mortal thing.

LES: And all for what? To leave our life's work on the linkroads for gippoes to plunder?

(JAMES *has been at boot of car and now returns with gun under arm.*)

JAMES: Les, with respect, let us ask ourselves: what is the essence of a first-rate civilization? The kind you and I earnestly crave? Surely it is that the greatest number of choices is given to the greatest number of citizens. Ever-proliferating democratic profusion. In other words, the free way. Now obviously such an infinity of options must remain an ideal; obviously too we must aim at nothing less. Neither the holy writ of the Marxist, nor the Luddite austerities of the Scrubber but the controlled chaos of parliamentary democracy. Not icy water but hot punch, not thin gruel but bouillabaisse.

BARRY: That's what I said. Or meant to.

JAMES: Now the Freeway has its weaknesses as well as its enemies and we may sometimes have to leave it to serve it. So that the fabric may be strengthened, the rules reappraised. And during the weeks ahead, while the Freeway is out of service, while the government exercises its emergency powers, there may be hardship, discomfort, danger, death. But, Les, you and I know it's only a skirmish in the battle for a free way that works. And knowing that, we who believe the Freeway to be the right way see no other course but to find our own ways home. The alternative is the dead end of despotism, a one-way street to a new age of darkness. (*To* LES.) I beg you——

LES: And what about the Wreckers?

JAMES: They'll get what they're asking, won't they, Minister?

BARRY: I dare say. We can't build without first knocking down. (*Thunder. People look at the sky. One of the officers speaks aside to* BARRY.)
Yes, right. The helicopter's waiting, I must fly. *Arrividerci*, James. *A bientôt.*

JAMES: Very well.

BARRY: Bye, bye, ladies and gentlemen, chaps and chapesses. I'm going to tell the Prime Minister you may be down in the mouth but you're not downhearted. In fact, you're in jolly good nick. What are you?

CROWD (*feebly*): In jolly good nick.
(BARRY *goes to back, where* SOLDIERS *clear a way.*)
And remember the TV cameras will be following you on the Long Walk. So give us a smile and a wave and show them what kind of people you are, eh? Tally-ho!

CROWD: Tally-ho!
(*As he makes exit followed by his retinue,* CROWD *drifts away,*

including SCALES, *who collect stuff from boot of car.*)

MAY (*to* EVELYN): All very well for him with his three Rolls-Royces.

JAMES: Appalling luck, though, this happening during his Ministry. And not really his fault. Indeed, looked at closely, nothing is ever anyone's fault.

MAY: Nobody's fault?

(COX *leads* JAMES *aside.*)

LES (*to* MAY): Don't interfere in politics, love.

MAY: Oh, lovely. (*To* EVELYN.) Stand in the corner with a dunce's cap on.

LES: I didn't mean that, but—d'you agree with James or not?

MAY: What you asking me for? You told me not to interfere.

EVELYN: I don't think you need to understand. It's more his way of talking.

(JAMES *has gone off, right, with* COX. *Only* LES, MAY, EVELYN *remain.*

Thunder, LES *looks up.*)

LES: I suppose I better strike this tent.

MAY: Wally!

(WALLY *has come along downstage of fence, stooping to avoid being seen, now he rolls under and they help him up. We see that his clothes are bloodstained and the sleeve of his jacket torn. Face bruised, muddy.*)

EVELYN: You're bleeding.

WALLY: Ain't my blood. Had to kill a dog. I was down the dairy unit, got us a bowl of cream . . . just coming away and one of those crazy Alsatians come at me. Got hold of my arm but I done for him with this—

(*Shows knife, stuck in belt.*)

MAY: My steak knife.

WALLY: Lost the cream but I got these.

(*Shows two green apples.* EVELYN *goes into bus.*)

MAY: Don't risk your life. We're not starving.

WALLY: Not yet, but this ain't gonna be no picnic from now on. There's armed Rangers all over. A couple of them come after me, that dog made so much noise dying.

MAY: Haven't you heard, though, love? We've got to take up our beds and walk.

WALLY: I heard, yeah. I been lying in the ditch waiting for the soldiers to go.

LES: Only reasonable, only way to solve the crisis. As you say, it wouldn't be any picnic staying here.

WALLY: You're selling out again, Les.

LES: What's that?

WALLY: You've got too much to lose, I guess. A photo album, a Motor Home, a toilet-tent——

LES: You're not going to start on that again? Blimey O'Riley! (EVELYN *comes back with Red Cross box and dresses wound.*)

EVELYN: You're only grazed.

WALLY: Got him before he could sink his teeth in. Like a reflex action. Ain't had to kill since the war but seems I ain't forgot.

EVELYN: You never told me you were in the war.

LES: You get on my top-note, you do. Calling me a scab.

WALLY: Did I call you a——

LES: Accusing me of breaking solidarity with the lads in the other unions, then saying you don't give a monkey's for them anyway. What kind of solidarity's that? And you heard that Minister: they'll get their money.

WALLY: And what kind of victory's that? They'll get their money and buy all manner of crap and wreck the place they live and buy some goddam car and drive off and wreck some other place.

MAY: Oh, Wally, for goodness sake.

EVELYN: Nice language, I must say.

WALLY: Until they've wrecked the whole planet. And what then? Every family its own spacecraft?

LES: You're a bleeding malcontent, d'you know that?

MAY: Always has been. Even as a boy. Never learnt to march in step, did you?

WALLY: I watched the greedy bastards run the world. And I watched them turn the rest into greedy bastards too. Like a plague it's been, except not with rats but money.

EVELYN: If it's a plague, there's nothing to be done then, is there?

83

WALLY: Quit running. Stay where you are. Make it work, wherever you happen to be.

EVELYN: D'you mean stay here? This God-forsaken place? With all the nasty smells and insects in the food and no facilities?

(*Thunder.* WALLY *looks at her, offers her apple.*)

I'll share it out. Thank you.

LES: Come on, before this breaks. And, Wally, you help. No skiving, I know you.

(*Goes into tent.* EVELYN *packs away first aid, takes box into bus.* WALLY *stands, looking at his dressed wound.* MAY *goes to fold chairs, etc. During the next scene, these four clear: tent, pedal-bin, chairs, table, anything else that's left.* LES *goes upstage of bus with lavatory bucket.* RHYNES *return from right with* COX.)

JAMES (*offering hand to* LES): Les, may I say what a tremendous pleasure and privilege it's been, sharing this experience with you. And do let's meet again before too long. The House will always find me.

LES: Which house is that?

JAMES: The one beside Big Ben.

(PAYNE *emerges on top of Motor Home.* NANCY *and* COX *go behind.*)

Where we conduct the friendly tug-of-war between the apparently different interests of your faction and mine. For wasn't it Burke who said that parties must ever exist in a free country? I think you'll find it was.

(*Bids good-bye to the others as* NANCY *arrives on roof with* COX.)

MAY: What are you doing on our roof?

NANCY: Good-bye. Thank you for all your splendid help. I only wish we could stay. But we've our duty as well.

(*Helicopter approaches, arriving overhead with usual effects. A rigid ladder or cradle descends from the flies over the bus and* COX *and* PAYNE *help* NANCY *to climb up.* JAMES *has followed them on to the roof, still with gun. Speaks down to* LES, *watching on ground, raising his voice above the din.*)

JAMES: Les!

LES: Hallo?

JAMES: May I commend to you one last observation? It is from John Stuart Mill. "The only freedom which deserves the name is that of pursuing our own good in our own way, so long as we do not attempt to deprive others of theirs, or impede their efforts to obtain it."

(He follows his mother into the sky. Helicopter flies off as everyone waves. COX and PAYNE get off the roof and others resume their packing. WALLY does not reappear.

Thunder.

COX and PAYNE come to help.)

COX: Give you a hand with the Big Top, sir?

LES: Thanks.

COX: So you can get off toot-sweet.

LES: We haven't been given the word yet, officially.

COX *(shrugs)*: Sooner you move, the sooner you'll be there, the better your position in the queue. Sooner you'll get home and put the kettle on. Take only essential baggage of course, no articles of sentimental value, which could represent a temptation to roving lorry-drivers.

LES: D'you mean we're going on the motorways?

COX: I don't think you're going by Jumbo jet.

PAYNE: You'll be allocated to various pick-up points where hundreds of voluntary helpers will take you in every available form of transport to regional dispersal centres.

COX: They've been appealing on the radio for anything that moves on wheels . . . from a push-bike to a cattle-truck.

LES: Blimey O'Riley.

COX: You'll be all right. Remember nineteen-forty? The little craft?

LES: We had to leave the equipment behind on that occasion too.

(COX and LES clear tent and stow it. Verge is as it was at start, but for the rubbish piled downstage. GRANT and TRACY have got their baggage and locked their boot. MAY and EVELYN come from bus wearing anoraks, etc., carrying bags, umbrella, radio, ciné-camera. SCALES wave good-bye.)

GRANT: Making an early start. Bye-bye. See you later

perhaps.

MAY: Good-bye. See you on the ice.

TRACY (*to children, off*): Now don't fight, Sholto. Daddy's going to start us off. Right?

GRANT (*singing, as they go*): *I'll give you one-oh.*

BOTH: *Green grow the rushes-oh—*

MAY: Bless their hearts.

PAYNE (*to* EVELYN): Haven't you got more practical shoes? Or boots?

EVELYN: We only came for the day!

MAY: How far shall we have to walk then?

PAYNE: Anything up to ten miles.

EVELYN: Oh, my Lord!

(LES *has been round bus, locks door.*)

LES: Seen Wally?

MAY: He's the Missing Link.

LES: Ask him to do a stroke of work, he always does the vanishing trick.

COX: You'll meet him at the dispersal centre.

(LES *locks door of Motor Home, gives keys to* COX.)

LES: But he'd be useful on the road.

MAY: Perhaps we ought to wait for him.

COX: I shouldn't advise that. You'd best be cutting along. (*As* LES *makes to reply.*) Before the rain.

MAY: Your windcheater, love, and camera . . .

LES: Ta. Last shot of you against the Cherokee. Never know when we'll see it again. Come on, Evelyn, you know where to stand.

(*Women pose while* LES *runs camera.*)

COX: I should go now, if I were you, sir, not the middle of next week.

LES: Right you are.

(LES *brings keys to* COX *and gives him a banknote also.*)

See they take good care of her, will you, Sergeant?

COX: Do my best, sir. Thank you very much.

(*Women wait while* LES *goes to bus and rubs off a speck of dirt with his finger.*)

Bye-bye.

PAYNE: *Bon-voyage!*
>   (LES, MAY *and* EVELYN *go right.* COX *yawns, stretches, holds up other keys.*)
COX: Look. Lord Muck's keys. Nice little job lined up there. Driving to his game lodge. You on?
PAYNE: What about all that lot in front?
COX: Yes, well, after that lot's shunted into a car-park somewhere. See the Highlands before it disappears. Last countryside in Britain. We time it right, we might get dinner. You ever tasted venison?
>   (*They make off, left. More thunder.*
>
>   WALLY *looks through window of Cherokee. Opens door, comes out, shuts behind him. Wears parka, has knives which he stows about his person. Finishes one of the apples, throws down core, in pile of rubbish. He rearranges the wood pigeon in an airways bag round his neck.*)
WALLY (*sings, to himself*): *So what care I for my goose-feather bed*
>   *With the sheet turned down so bravely-oh—*
>   *Tonight I shall sleep in the cold open field—*
>   (*Crash of thunder as* WALLY *puts up his hood and drops to roll under fence. Hear rain falling heavily.*)

CURTAIN